THE VICTORIAN DOLLHOUSE BOOK

THE VICTORIAN DOLLHOUSE BOOK

NICK FORDER

CHARTWELL
BOOKS, INC.

A QUINTET BOOK

Published by Chartwell Books
A Division of Book Sales, Inc.
114 Northfield Avenue
Edison, New Jersey 08837

ISBN 0-7858-0566-4

This book was designed and produced by
Quintet Publishing Limited
6 Blundell Street
London N7 9BH

Creative Director: Richard Dewing
Designer: Ian Hunt
Project Editor: Anna Briffa
Editor: Alison Leach
Photographer: Jeremy Thomas

Typeset in Great Britain by
Central Southern Typesetters, Eastbourne
Manufactured in Malaysia by
C.H. Colourscan Sdn. Bhd.
Printed in China by Leefung-Asco Printers Ltd

ACKNOWLEDGMENTS

This book is dedicated to Esther, my loving wife,
without whose support, encouragement, advice, and
tolerance I would have been lost.

CONTENTS

PART I

PART II

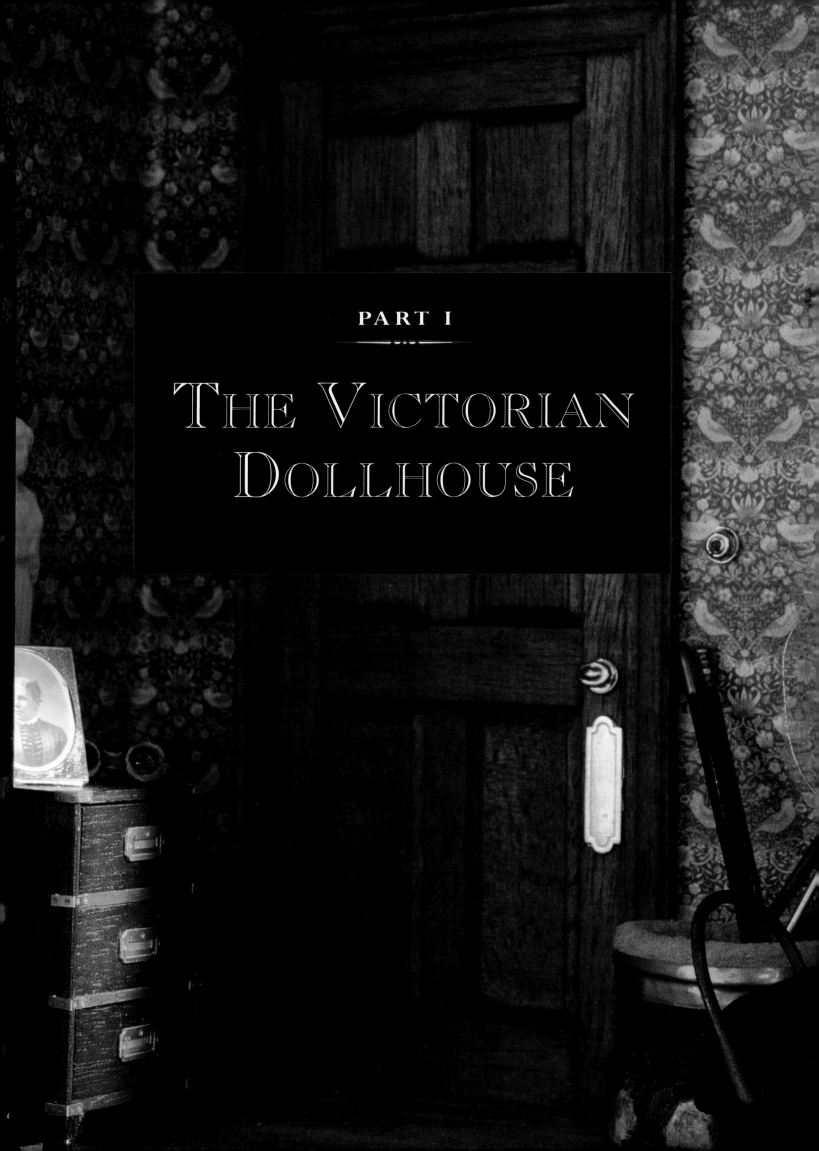

PART I

THE VICTORIAN DOLLHOUSE

INTRODUCTION

Perhaps the most popular concept of an ideal dollhouse is an elaborate Victorian plaything, encapsulating memories of childhood, images of eras gone by, and fantasy places. A dollhouse belongs to childhood or everyone's yesterday.

For those who enjoy the fascinating pastime of collecting dollhouses and miniatures, these concepts become the wings with which the miniaturist's mind can fly.

Although now modelers enjoy recreating a whole myriad of themes from medieval dungeons to penthouse suites, garden retreats to Bar Mitzvah celebrations, the most consistently popular time setting is somewhere within the idyllic-seeming Victorian age.

A dollhouse or miniature creation classified as "Victorian" has in fact a considerable amount of leeway. Historically, it is a period that lasted over 60 years – Queen Victoria reigned from 1837 until 1901 – and, in the field of interior decoration, perhaps some 10 or 12 years longer since design tastes evolved rather than just started and stopped in accordance with the length of the Queen's reign. Nevertheless, although popular taste altered frequently and wildly, the era combined some new concepts with traditional designs, taking the best and reshaping them into novel forms which latterly became known as Victorian.

This book celebrates this style in $\frac{1}{12}$ scale and shows examples of how a Victorian home, with all its glorious aspects, can be recreated in miniature. Within contemporary dollhouses and room boxes, each room of a Victorian home is recreated, illustrating differing styles found in different locations but all from the mid- to the end of the nineteenth century. In each case the influence is explained. Taken room by room, important contents are discussed separately, with advice and guidance on how the effects can be achieved. Alongside the main room settings other rooms of similar function but different style are shown. In addition a number of alternative pieces of furniture are illustrated separately to show differing designs but all are categorized as Victorian.

RIGHT *Furniture from Oberon's study in Titania's Palace, Legoland; a smoker's table, a cello, an armchair and a bowl of shrub roses.*

LEFT *A number of the British rooms featured in this book are set within this elegant double-fronted doll's house. The bay windows, central door, half basement, and dormer windows in the roof are all typical details found on numerous town houses built in the* nineteenth century. *The railings, too, are a perfect touch but most real houses are without them now, as they were removed during World War Two for melting down in order to produce ammunition. Interesting to note is the existence of a Sun Fire Office Plaque.* Introduced as early as 1710, in the days of private fire services, they were found on houses covered by the Sun Fire Office. They were still issued until about 1860.

The Victorian Era

Before looking at the rooms in detail it might be helpful to consider the period itself in order to understand the different fashions apparent in interior decoration. The nineteenth century saw an enormous degree of social change. Britain became strong and confident in possession of a powerful empire, and life on the American continent was well established with ample opportunity for individual self-improvement. Consequently, the middle classes expanded. They no longer worked at home but went to offices, factories, and other business premises, resulting in greater production and efficiency. Their increased earning power enabled them to achieve comfortable surroundings in their homes; treasure houses to display a mélange of taste and wealth. For such people family life was all-important.

To satisfy this desire for possessions, mass production made goods in all manner of historical, then known as revival, styles. By and large it was Britain which influenced both taste and style for as yet the United States were young and inexperienced in the field of home decoration. However, confidence quickly grew and unique interpretations developed particularly on the west coast. Between 1830 and 1900 a number of style revivals and movements related to design played a part in the resulting varied, eclectic mixture that is termed Victorian.

It may be that the period should be subdivided as, naturally, popular fashion shifted as time moved on. American Empire, Gothic, Elizabethan, rococo, Renaissance, and Grecian Egyptian were all styles exploited, while art from India, Turkey, Persia, China, and Japan coexisted under the generic term "oriental." Later new principles laid down by Charles L. Eastlake and William Morris led to simpler interiors and then to more arts-and-crafts-related ones. Evolving from the neoclassical forms that were popular from 1790 to the 1830s, American Empire, Gothic, Elizabethan, and rococo revivals were the furnishing styles that would fall into the first part of the era. Nostalgic, traditional, picturesque, and romantic, these were the qualities that appealed to the early Victorian.

The year 1851 saw the Great Exhibition held in London's Hyde Park. Supported by Queen Victoria and even more enthusiastically by her consort Albert, this famous exhibition encouraged the advancement in man's technical and artistic achievement that was to be displayed to all. Elaborately designed objects were brought from all around the world and although the exhibition had its critics, it heralded a new age of design. Often referred to as high Victorian, this subdivision of the era was possibly the longest lasting, continuing some 25 years. This period perhaps gives rise to popular notions of what is Victorian. Against backgrounds in Renaissance and rococo styles the emphasis was on possessions and home comfort. Everything was decorated and no space was left unadorned.

By 1875 reaction had set in — reaction against interiors dominated by overbearing decoration and clutter. Although overlapped by high Victorian, the last quarter of the century marks the final division of the period. In 1872 Charles L. Eastlake wrote a book entitled *Hints on Household Taste*. In it he decried design principles and the excesses of the previous 30 years, advocating simpler, less adorned elements of style. Initially this led merely to less flamboyant interiors but eventually to those of a more "aesthetic" taste. Rooms became more casual and simple, even slightly Bohemian but at the same time more coordinated There was a look back to the previous century in the reign of Queen Anne but with a less formal air, whilst handcrafted items were once again preferred to those mass produced. Queen Victoria, who gave her name to this period of contrasting styles, died in 1901 but in design the influences of her time continued for some years, particularly in the United States where revivals persisted.

OPPOSITE, ABOVE *A Victorian bedroom, conceivably from the San Francisco area. The window alcove's fretworked top, the tiered wall shelf and the lidded vase are all in the oriental taste so prevalent on America's west coast.*

OPPOSITE, BELOW *A linoleum floor, shelves displaying decorative china, and stored food, handy for immediate use, were all familiar aspects of the "new kitchen" which evolved after America's Civil War.*

THE VICTORIAN HOUSE

With the new significance in the importance of their homes, the middle classes gave enormous attention to furnishing and decoration. Magazines and books on household decorative design and etiquette were available for guidance as so many aspects were involved in creating the desired impression. For those new classes whose home no longer doubled as a work place, it took on another meaning. Now it became a sanctuary, a safe haven from the world outside, and comfort was essential. This, together with a degree of convention and a wish to reflect status and show overt signs of new wealth, made the home a monument to family and achievement.

However, this separation of work and home created a gulf in the occupations of men and women. Whilst men earned the money, women remained at home. It was a wife's task to manage the house and indeed all this adhered to the Victorian ideal. Increasingly male and female roles became clearly defined and nowhere were they more observed than within the home, to the extent that rooms became designated as masculine or feminine domains and were decorated in accordance. For example, areas used for social or family life, such as the drawing room, parlor, or conservatory, were thought feminine and furnished decoratively, whereas the hall, dining room (sometimes doubling as a smoking room after dinner), and the study were considered masculine and were decorated in a more appropriately serious, somber mode.

So it followed that in larger houses which might have a ballroom and boudoirs, these would be decorated in feminine taste, whereas libraries, a billiard room, or separate smoking room would, in turn, be masculine. Kitchens, sculleries, and servants' bedrooms were furnished purely functionally as these were merely the province of those of a lower class. Children again were allocated separate areas within the house but here too it was often deemed necessary to segregate the sexes.

The arrangement of living space in a new middle-class home was clearly a complex business, not eased by aspirations toward a more aristocratic lifestyle. Home entertaining was most important and the drawing and main reception rooms were the ideal places to display to guests their hosts' wealth and excellent taste. At the same time family privacy became increasingly sought and separate family rooms developed. Naturally the ideal was to have a separate room for each function, each furnished appropriately.

ABOVE *A real-life reconstruction of a mid-Victorian parlor. The furnishings are all typical of the style.*

ABOVE *From the San Francisco Bay area this model hallway captures many important features. The tripartite wall, the oriental decoration, the entrance door with side lights and the archway, open to the next room are Victorian features that establish the room.*

LEFT *Dark somber decoration and ecclesiastical details are the elements that are the foundation for this Gothic style study. Note the glimmer of light that passes from the window.*

VICTORIAN STYLE IN MINIATURE

Just as there was no one particular style that was incorporated into every Victorian home in reality, so it would not be possible, or even desirable, to recreate one in miniature. Before beginning a project, it might therefore be better to select a specific date from the era or, at least, from one of the subdivisions: early, middle, or late Victorian. Having done that, the location should be chosen, together with an idea of imaginary inhabitants. If a whole dollhouse is to be decorated and furnished in Victorian style, the exterior of the house should determine a number of these points.

Today many makers specialize in creating ½-scale crafted pieces based on Victorian designs, while miniature wallpaper, moldings, and building supplies are all readily available through mail order, shows, and miniature stores. An existing collection of miniatures may inspire a new project, in which case this also might dictate the particular period in which the miniature scene should be set. Whichever of the styles is selected, good references are essential for it is accuracy that is a major factor in creating a successful miniature.

WORK MATERIALS

Before starting to execute a project, a few basic tools, at least, will be needed: sandpaper, in fine and medium grades, for use on dollhouse walls and furniture alike; a sharp craft knife and extra blades for cutting wallpaper and trimming kits; a measuring rule; a metal straight edge; and of course a pencil. For slightly more advanced work, the following will also be needed: a modeler's saw and miter block for cutting baseboards, architraves, and other moldings; a small drill for making wiring holes; and perhaps a jigsaw for cutting doorways, fireplaces, and windows. Finally, for decoration, small paintbrushes and artist's brushes are needed for paint work and wood-staining, crack filler for uneven corners or discrepancies in the woodwork, wood glue, and a pot of wallpaper paste. Keeping tools in a housekeeping tidy might be a good idea, particularly if there is enough space for a construction and cutting board. It is hoped that the room settings shown on the following pages will act not only as a guide to varying Victorian styles but also as a source of inspiration for creating dollhouse miniatures.

1872 "Penfold" pillar box designed by an architect of that name. Originally this style of box was painted green.

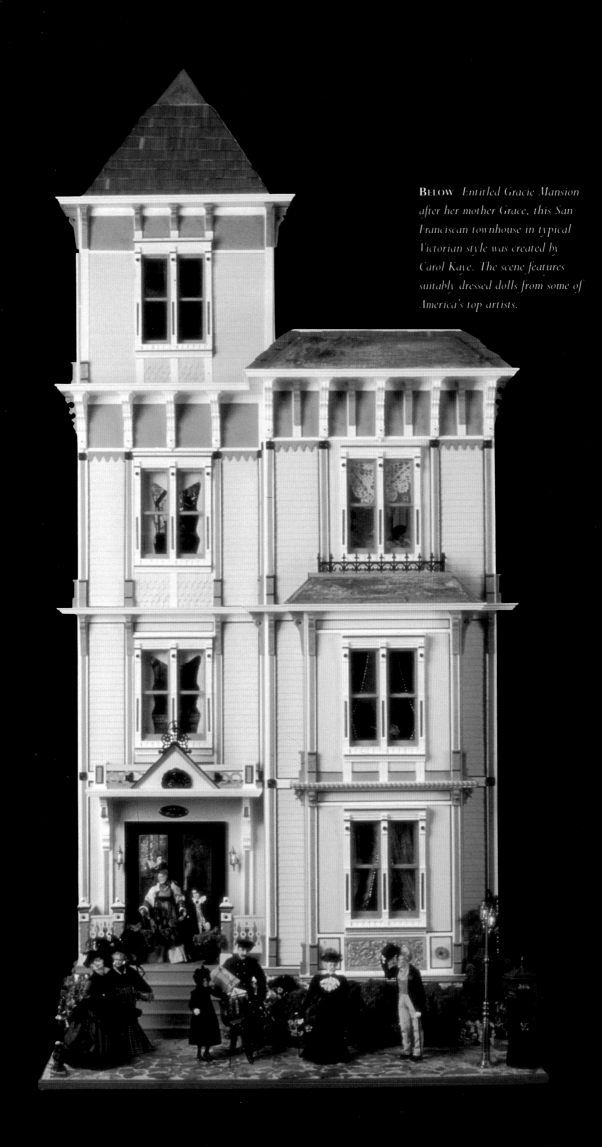

BELOW *Entitled Gracie Mansion after her mother Grace, this San Franciscan townhouse in typical Victorian style was created by Carol Kaye. The scene features suitably dressed dolls from some of America's top artists.*

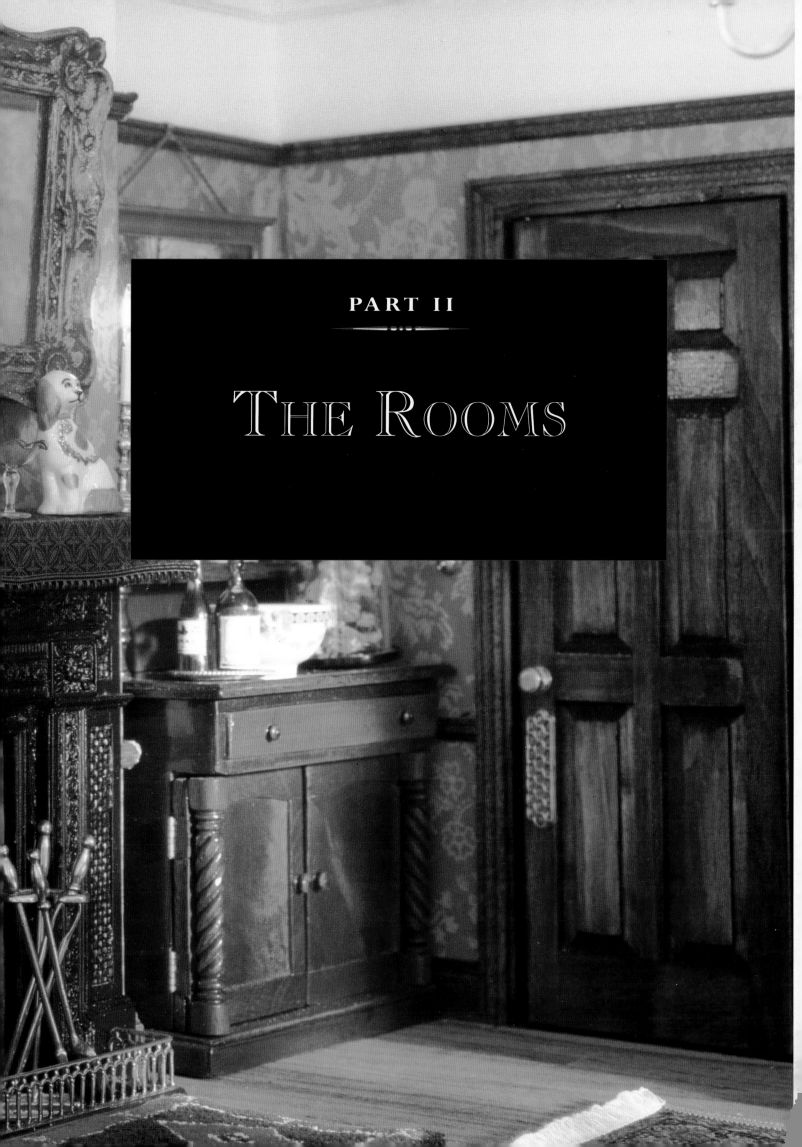

PART II

THE ROOMS

KEY FEATURES IN A HALLWAY

Towards the end of the century tastes became less stuffy and Americans favored more informal styles of decoration. The tripartite wall was one that was divided into three: the bottom third of one design, a central field area of another, and a patterned frieze terminating in the cornice at the top. This west coast hallway created in ½ scale has been decorated in such a fashion. The woodwork including the hardwood floor is still dark but the overall effect is nevertheless much lighter than that in halls of earlier decades.

The love of the oriental, most prevalent on the west coast, is another feature of this hallway. The lidded jars, hall table, plant table, door rug, and vase are all in keeping. To the right of the door on entry is a grand hallway piece with wall shelf supported on ornate brackets with a large framed mirror hung above. Another typical feature is a view through to the drawing room, which is also decorated in oriental style. Plants, flowers, umbrella stand, grandfather clock, and a

silver tray on the hall table complete the hall's furnishings, while the lithophane-shaded table lamp is particularly novel.

This room was constructed in conjunction with the drawing room in order to create the room-to-room vistas so typical of the date. Before the precut walls, floor, and ceiling were constructed, holes were cut to accommodate the ready-made door with its glazed sidelights, the stairway, and the arch that leads to the next room. When completed, the box could be assembled and the ceiling painted cream. Ready-made miniature moldings for the cornice, dado rail, architraves, and baseboard, together with components for the staircase, arch decorations, and the doorway, were stained in a rich Victorian mahogany and subsequently varnished.

LEFT *A view from the back of the house towards the front door. The drawing room can be seen through an arched doorway.*

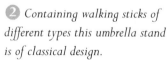

2 *Containing walking sticks of different types this umbrella stand is of classical design.*

1 *Stags, deer, and other beasts of prey were popular with Victorians, who incorporated them into all manner of decorative items. This miniature is handcrafted from bronze.*

THE HALL

Initial impressions often count the most and it is the entrance hall that visitors see first. The Victorians were aware that their home would be seen as a reflection of themselves and it must therefore display all signs of wealth and social status. The hall was given as much, if not more, decorative attention as other rooms used for entertaining and the reception of visitors.

At the start of the period the hallway seemed less important, serving merely as the initial shelter from the outside world that in turn led to more functional areas of the house. As time went by and home entertaining became the vogue, halls became grander and more impressive. By the end of the century good-size homes boasted much larger halls with perhaps fireplaces, built-in niches, and curtained archways that part-screened glimpses of the splendors that lay within further rooms. To a degree the hallway became an addition to the drawing room. A hallway was desired in even modest homes; such space distinguished it from a working-class home that had none at all.

To create the right impression, halls were rather dark and somber but nevertheless they were another area for display. A home owner would like visitors to feel a sense of substance, security, sensibility, and a little awe. Later the halls were furnished well but never really comfortably because welcome visitors would be ushered immediately into the drawing room. Only tradespeople or servants might actually wait in the hall. Important people who were not expected might just leave a calling card.

The necessary furniture required would include racks for hats, coats, canes, and umbrellas. Huge oversize stands that incorporated accommodation for all these were very popular, often including, in addition, a mirror, glove box, and lidded seat compartment in a single piece of furniture. Other pieces might be straight-backed chairs, hall tables, benches or stools, and perhaps a heavily carved chest.

Accessories were selected with considerable care. Flower vases, a barometer, wildlife sculptures, and of course the visiting card tray were all considered appropriate. Family pictures or small etchings were acceptable in the hall with a few larger paintings of subjects not considered too thought-provoking – the idea being that paintings worthy of study and appreciation should be hung elsewhere where they could be enjoyed for longer periods of time.

ABOVE *From the* Guthrie Collection *miniature display at Hever Castle in England this small part of a front hall demonstrates the grandeur of a Victorian country house. The Gothic theme is carried out in the architectural details of moldings and ceiling. Below the dado rail is embossed wallpaper known as anaglypta.*

④

CONTEMPORARY BRITISH STYLE

By contrast this British-style hall is based on a suburban house of the 1850s to 1890s. The floor of red and buff tiles, arranged in a geometric pattern, is typical of the period. Typical also is the dark woodwork, the Lincrusta-embossed relief paper used for the dado, and stained-glass-patterned window set within the door. The use of embossed papers, sometimes giving the effect of leather, was particularly popular in the last two decades of the nineteenth century.

The Great Exhibition of 1851 had such an impact on the six million people who visited the subsequently named Crystal Palace that souvenirs and memorabilia could be found in numerous British homes. One such example was the original of the wallpaper used in this hallway. In shades of green and brown are scenes of the Serpentine in London's Hyde Park with the Crystal Palace looming beyond, all set within a "frame" of an ornate rural gateway. In keeping too are the hall table, replete with ornaments and visiting card tray, the cast-iron umbrella stand, the mahogany balloon-backed chair, and the jardiniere with growing plant.

To create this hall (set within a commercially made dollhouse), the first task was to paint the ceiling, including a ceiling rose about 1½ inches below the cornice. A pencil line was drawn around the walls at the levels of the dado and picture rails. This was to determine the distance between the two, as again reduced, photocopied papers were to be used. With careful adjustment of the photocopier, enough pieces of an illustration of Heywood, Higginbottom, and Smith designs of 1853–55 to pattern-match correctly were reproduced and fitted exactly between the rails. After hanging the papers, the floor of prelaid separate tiles were glued into place. These tiles are made by Terry Curran who produces quite a variety of individual tiles. By cutting a piece of card, or thin plastic, to the exact size of the floor, the tiles can be arranged and cemented onto the card which can, in turn, be put inside the room. The floor should then be varnished and later grouted. With walls, ceiling, and floor completed, prestained architraves, baseboards, picture and dado rails can all be mitered and fitted to the room. Twelve-volt lights are fitted as before and with furniture, accessories, and plants in place, pictures, a mirror, and a barometer were added.

RIGHT *The detailing of this narrow hallway is quintessentially British. Note the design of the ceramic-tiled floor, balloon-backed chair and the wallpaper design, based on the Great Exhibition of 1851.*

❶ *Two bronze figures on marble bases. These are British and were made by Tony Knott.*

❷ *Decorative plant pots on matching stands were almost obligatory, finding space in hallways, drawing rooms, studies, and dining rooms alike.*

❸ *Known as balloon-backed this type of chair was immensely popular. This model was made from a metal kit and finished to represent wood.*

Paper then followed in the manner of the three-part wall. Firstly, for the bottom 3 inches, a design was reduced and reproduced on a photocopier with enough copies made so that, when carefully pattern-matched and trimmed, there was enough to go around the room. Then one ready-made dollhouse wallpaper was chosen for the "field" and another, from which the frieze was taken, and in turn pasted onto the walls. When all was dry, the staircase and doorway, with its previously fitted "etched glass," were assembled and stuck into position. Architrave, cornice, and dado rail were then cut from the prestained wood and mitered to fit around the room. The floor was trimmed to size from a ready-made miniature floorboard sheet and, when stuck down, sandpapered and treated with floor polish. The

baseboard could then be cut to size and glued into place.

For lighting, 12-volt fixtures were chosen and their wires fed through holes drilled through the ceiling and the wall. For a more authentic look, a plaster ceiling rose was chosen and, when aligned, the chandelier's wires were passed through the holes in both rose and ceiling. These in turn were soldered to parallel copper tapes of a lighting system.

Ready-made furniture and accessories had been chosen in keeping with the room but frequently it is possible to create something original quite simply. For the wall shelf below the mirror a plaster top from a miniature bench was taken and after being painted gray, small irregular lines of black and white were brushed on to give the effect of marble veins. The supports are a pair of corbels intended for outside use. When gilded, they complete a lovely pier table.

LEFT *On the staircase side of the hall the tripartite wall can be seen more clearly. The dado paper has patterns of stylized irises, sunbursts and geometric borders. The main "field" paper is a reproduction of a paper taken from an old dollhouse from the middle of the nineteenth century. The lamp with lithophane shade is interesting too.*

LEFT *From across the hallway is a view into the drawing room. The oriental feel is echoed in the plant stand, rug, and lidded jars.*

4 This gold-colored pot with pretty leaf design is actually ceramic. The plant leaves are painted paper.

3 Handworked miniature items such as this rug show the intricacy of a miniaturist's work.

FURNISHINGS FROM THE HALLWAY

Gathered here are a number of pieces that might have been found in various hallways from the period. The small desk, shoe scrapers and doorstop would definitely be British, whilst the Eastlake sofa and combination hall stand are American, dating from late in the nineteenth century.

Small desk, side, or hall table. The turned legs are typical of Victorian styling.

A hall sofa in Eastlake style.

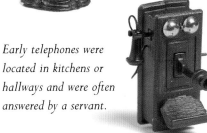

Two boot and shoe scrapers. The one on the left would be set into a wall outside the front door.

A Mr. Punch doorstop of cast iron.

Early telephones were located in kitchens or hallways and were often answered by a servant.

Grandfather clocks were an impressive addition to the hallway.

With mirror, lift-up seat, armrests, hooks, and a rack for walking sticks this hall stand suits a number of its purposes. It is late Victorian.

HALL STANDS

During the era hat, coat and umbrella stands varied considerably. Larger versions stood proudly in larger halls whilst smaller ones squeezed their way into small ones. Most styles adapted by the Victorians were applied to these essential assets to the hallway which appeared in wood, metals, ceramic, bamboo, marble and combinations of all of these.

This miniature brass umbrella stand contains an assortment of walking sticks.

Combination hall stand suitable for smaller halls.

An ornately styled umbrella stand. The original would have been in cast iron.

The original of this stand would have been made of bamboo but the miniature is skillfully painted metal.

Two pretty umbrellas that are handmade British.

Coat, hat, cane, and umbrella stands were essential items for the hall.

A simple umbrella stand that has an inset metal drip tray.

THE DRAWING ROOM

The drawing room takes its name from the room to which ladies withdrew, leaving the gentlemen at the table after dinner. It became the most important room of the house. Still furnished in an essentially feminine style, this room was usually also the largest, boasting grander windows, more elaborate moldings, and greater ornamentation of cornices on the higher ceilings. Used as the main reception room and entertaining area, this was the setting in which to impress visitors. Here the most costly furnishings were employed, utilizing yard upon yard of fabric often overlaid and fringed for curtains, seating, tables, mantel shelves, and even architectural moldings alike, often in the same color but in varying degrees of tone. Items of female choosing prevailed with styles of drapery, plumages, and floral arrangement so similar to that of ladies' personal dress.

Tapestry work and needlepoint were put to a number of uses in the drawing room. In more modest middle-class homes where the parlor would be the main room, a lady's own handicrafts might be displayed within the room. Where a drawing room existed, such work would probably be relegated to a second family parlor or a lady's private boudoir. Frequently the drawing room would be crammed with furniture not only for purposes of display but also to offer plenty of seating, often arranged in a number of small groupings within the room.

Center tables were most popular with subsidiary tables surrounded by the chairs. In turn these tables were bedecked with a mass of carefully placed decorative and novel items intended to stimulate

ABOVE *A drawing room of Gothic revival style by John Hodgson. The wallpaper is of a William Morris design of 1877 entitled Bower. The traditional wood floor is covered by a copy of an authentic Aubusson carpet.*

conversation. In addition pier tables, étagères and whatnots, cabinets, and curio shelves, all groaned under the weight of framed photographs, vases, statuary, urns, plants, bowls, endless stuffed creatures under glass domes, and all manner of purposeless objets d'art, all vying for attention.

Suites of furniture comprising a sofa, pier and center tables, and a number of parlor chairs became popular from about the middle of the century but losing favor again by the end. Still dominating the room would be an ornate fireplace. Above this most often hung a mirror. Set in a wide decorative frame, the mirror might seem even larger than it was. The effect of a mirror of good size was that it made a room appear even more spacious and effectively doubled the quantity of treasures it reflected. Later in the period fire mantels, mirrors, and surrounding shelves became incorporated into one having a more immediate effect on objects placed within it. Fire screens, canterburys, plant stands, teapoys, work tables – the list of furniture found in a drawing room was endless, for the more important the room was the more furniture it should have within it. The idea was that the larger quantity of possessions displayed within the room suggested the family's greater wealth and stature.

Art was widely appreciated and a good collection of paintings, preferably original or commissioned, served as examples of a person's good taste and culture as well as inviting conversation. The walls of the drawing room, as the most important reception room, would be hung with the home owner's best pictures.

INSPIRATION FROM CHINA

Slightly earlier than the adjoining hallway would be the date of this drawing room with its walls papered all in one color and with a decorative frieze around the top. Furnishings would have been termed oriental, being either from China or Chinese-inspired.

The glazed cabinet, shelves, vase stands, and tables are all in the Chinese style. Blue and white china, known as willow ware through its most popular design, was avidly collected – nowhere more than on the west coast, even though it became vastly over-produced by the late 1840s. One of the most important features of the room is, however, the miniature collection of blue and white porcelain. The Victorians loved collecting, particularly in themes and this they have in common with the miniaturists today. The pieces collected here are from varying crafts people. The fireplace with a mass of shelves and a built-in mirror is perfectly suited to the display of porcelain pieces, while other decorative items found homes inside the cabinet, on shelves, and on table tops for maximum visual effect.

Embroidered and needlepoint fabrics were also extremely popular. Here such work has been put to use on a three-piece sofa set with matching stool. Also of a feminine taste are the pictures that adorn the walls depicting young ladies, children, babies, and family photographs.

The ceiling has been painted an off-white and the woodwork stained mahogany. The wallpaper is specially made for dollhouses and is fairly easy to find. The floor, also of parquet design, is produced in $\frac{1}{12}$ scale and can be cut and trimmed to fit the room. As before, decoration was carried out in sequence; starting with ceiling painting, through wallpapering and flooring, and finally fitting the architraves and molding. Lights were connected in the usual way.

To furnish, Chinese pieces from Bespaq were used. This furniture is actually made in China so was more than fitting for this room. The sofa set is also by Bespaq but this was supplied in an unvarnished state. After sandpapering and subsequent varnishing, the desired look for the framework of each piece was achieved. Panels were then cut from an old handbag and used to reupholster the set.

OVERLEAF *Overall the appearance of this room seems a little too heavy for the warmth and brightness of a San Francisco climate. However, such was the fashion of the second part of the nineteenth century. The influence of the orient was particularly popular.*

ABOVE *Created by miniature artisan Nic Nichols, this beautiful Victorian parlor is now on display in the Toy and Miniature Museum of Kansas City. Of particular interest are the archways, giving views to further areas, the ornate ceiling, the tasseled table, the carved button-backed sofa and chairs, and the elaborate ceiling oil lamp that helps establish the date.*

DRAWING ROOM FURNITURE

As with all pieces of Victorian furniture, adopted styles were interpreted in numerous different ways. Chairs, sofas and footstools were no exception and could be found in Regency or Classical variations to designs inspired by the writings of Charles Lock Eastlake.

Late-Victorian-style chair.

High-curved, button-backed sofas were popular for American drawing rooms and parlors.

Comfortable easy chair, suitably cushioned and well padded.

Heavily stuffed and buttoned, this miniature by John Hodgson looks most comfortable. It is made from resin, however, with its upholstery cleverly painted.

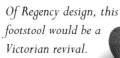

Of Regency design, this footstool would be a Victorian revival.

Simple piano or organ stool, maintaining the detail of turned legs.

Although Regency in style, this sofa might well be a Victorian revival.

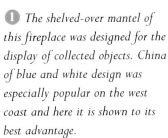

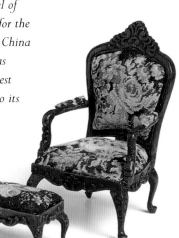

LEFT *Behind the fireplace a door leads to another room. Further oriental influence can be seen in the Chinese garden seat finished in antique stone.*

2 *A collection of Russian lacquer boxes fills the surface of this marble-topped "D" table with fanciful swan legs.*

1 *The shelved-over mantel of this fireplace was designed for the display of collected objects. China of blue and white design was especially popular on the west coast and here it is shown to its best advantage.*

3 *The needlepoint fabric for the chair and matching stool was "borrowed" from an antique evening bag.*

4 *Again in oriental style this "biblot" table holds a cloisonné vase.*

5 *Beautiful handmade flowers in Victorian style adorn this little side table.*

CABINETS FOR DISPLAY AND SHOW

The open display of one's wealth and standing was achieved through the amount of collected objects one possessed. Interesting pieces of glass, silver or porcelain in forms of vases, figurines, and dishes all had the influence to impress. This accounts for the popularity of glazed display cabinets, open shelf units and numerous curio cases and tables, all produced in various styles.

Another oriental hybrid. A style probably made for a Western market.

Glazed display and curio cabinets were also very popular. This one is designed to stand in a corner.

This hexagonal curio cabinet has a strong Gothic feel.

Gothic bookcase designed to be either freestanding or built into the wall.

Designed for standing on a shelf or cabinet top this curio cabinet has curved decoration and a small drawer.

This small wall or table cabinet measures only 2 inches.

ADDITIONS TO THE DRAWING ROOM

All manner of small pieces of furniture could be found in the drawing room for, as the main area in which to receive guests, this was also the place that should have most on display.

A canterbury of delicate yew wood. Originally they were used for music sheets but more recently for papers, magazines, and journals.

This little bookshelf also has space for music sheets and periodicals in its top.

For the storage of music sheets or papers this ornamental stand also has a drawer.

This Chinese chair is almost timeless but "oriental" furniture was much sought after in this era in particular.

The turned legs and carved arms on this rocker are identified as "American Victorian country."

Music stand with adjustable bookstand on a wooden ratchet.

Footstool of a late nineteenth century design.

Pretty arrangement of dried flowers protected under a glass dome.

Home craft portraying Victorian lower-middle-class sentimentality.

A basic footstool or step-up-stool of functional design.

ABOVE *The hall is visible from the drawing room.*
More oriental ware is on view, arranged within a
suitable display cabinet.

① *Wild animals encapsulated in settings under glass domes were very much de rigueur in both Britain and the United States. This one contains a handpainted owl.*

Even this glazed cabinet has oriental fretwork designs.

② *The bamboo design here is pierced through the porcelain.*

THE IMPORTANT CENTER TABLE

No drawing room or parlor would be complete without a table at its center acting almost as an altar containing the room's most precious possessions. If the room were larger there might be a number of such tables, often with each surrounded by chairs to form an intimate grouping. Where the room was smaller or of a secondary nature the central table might also be used for dining.

Top-opening and lockable, this curio table owes its design to former eras.

Glass paperweights are displayed within the top of this ideal Victorian form.

Queen-Anne-style drum curio table designed to hold smaller objects.

Small side table in Eastlake style. This miniature is made of plastic.

Round, heavy-based Victorian table, ideal for the center of the parlor.

Mahogany center table in Renaissance revival style, 1850–1870.

Round center table with decoration of grapes and fruits.

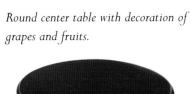

The gilded cage on this cloth-covered center table contains a miniature bird that actually sings.

PLANT STANDS AND ÉTAGÈRES

In addition to display or curio cabinets a number of smaller shelves and stands were developed. These were ideal for displaying smaller ornaments, busts and plants.

This four-tiered corner whatnot could have no function other than for display.

Multipurpose four-shelved whatnot complete with drawer.

Three-tiered whatnot or étagère.

A very decorative plant stand cast in metal.

Of bamboo structure and oriental in design, this cabinet would have been considered "aesthetic."

Plant stand from the late nineteenth century.

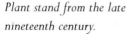

An early Charles Rennie Mackintosh piece. This miniature was made by Felton Miniatures.

An almost museum-like display of stuffed birds. A case like this, however, would have been from a private home.

The sinewy form of this plant stand is fashioned from wood.

NEW YORK STYLE

This drawing room (*overleaf*) took its inspiration from a model put together by Mrs. Thorne in the late 1930s based on the New York childhood home of Theodore Roosevelt. The house, it is said, dates from between 1850 and 1870.

The fireplace, mirror, ornate wall tables, and Belter furniture are features taken from the original room. John Henry Belter was the New York cabinetmaker who gave his name to the curve-backed, highly carved furniture that he developed. The miniature pieces of that style in the room are the two-seat sofa and two chairs beside the table. The remaining items of furniture would also have been from around the same period, as would the style of the drapes. Ornaments here are comparatively few but this is a room not of "new money."

Measuring 20 x 12 x 11 inches high, the construction of this room was relatively simple. A chimney breast of 1-inch depth was constructed to fit and located center back of the room. Prior to fitting, a hole for a fireplace was cut out to size. The cornice was then measured and mitered to fit. After the ceiling was painted, wallpaper was hung. The pattern used here is by Mini Graphics and coincidentally entitled "Roosevelt Rose". The floor is another sheet of fiberglass "parquet" cut to size and glued into place.

Prepainted baseboard and picture rail then followed suit with a chandelier and wall brackets by Small Time Operators, electrified as previously explained. The drapes and valance were especially made by expert Anne Ruff. These were then trimmed with gold braid and the valance topped with a gilded cornice. The picture frames, on heavy chains, were both ready-made miniatures and rummage sale finds. A postcard catalog from the National Gallery provided excellent prints to embellish the room. Finally, with furniture by Bespaq and Handcraft Designs and a rug from a new line from MacDoc Designs, the mood of the era has been faithfully reproduced.

OVERLEAF *Based on a previous miniature interpretation by Mrs. Thorne in the 1930s, this drawing room could have been from the New York childhood home of Theodore Roosevelt. Perhaps more restrained than other homes of the 1860s, it reflects that its owner was not newly wealthy.*

The two-seat sofa, or love seat, is in the Belter style.

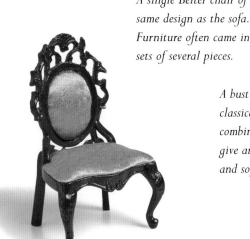

A single Belter chair of the same design as the sofa. Furniture often came in sets of several pieces.

A bust on a podium in classical style. Such combinations were used to give an air of knowledge and sophistication.

ABOVE *From the window, the sun falls across the floor to the opposite wall. The pictures, glass-domed ornament, and elaborate étagère are all of mid-Victorian taste.*

❶ *The ornate canterbury, originally designed for music, soon became used for the storage of periodicals and journals.*

❷ *Another creation under a glass dome. Often a home craft, this one would have been made by one of the ladies in the house.*

LEFT *The drapes and cornice were made especially for this room. Trimmings of contrasting colors, especially gold, were a much favored taste. Note the floor register on the left of the window.*

THE PARLOR

Essentially the parlor was rated beneath the drawing room. It was either the main reception room in a less well-to-do home or a less important, more intimate family room in a wealthier one. In order to create a greater flexibility of room usage in smaller houses, two or more parlors might be linked by folding or sliding pocket doors. These could be opened wide on special occasions to give the impression of one large drawing room.

Whether interconnecting or not, the apportioning of a front parlor for company and a back parlor for the family and close friends was an extremely popular solution. With a center table in position in the back parlor, this room might in turn double as a dining room. In terms of decoration the same criteria prevailed as those in the drawing room, albeit slightly more modestly. In smaller homes furniture would generally be simpler and less ornate, and the objets d'art of a lower quality.

Quantity rather than quality proved to be the rule in the parlor. Again a sofa, parlor chairs, assorted tables, étagères, chiffoniers, cabinets, dressers, upholstered chairs, and sometimes a piano or harmonium would all be suitable furnishings. Examples of embroidery or needlepoint along with crochet and lacework might be found on shelves and walls alike with the ubiquitous tid evident in both Britain and America. Collections of glass and chinaware were displayed with the usual Victorian pride, with goldfish in bowls and birds in cages also much favored.

ABOVE *Set c. 1840 this French New Orleans parlor was made by Eugene Kupjack in 1981 and is now on view at the* Carole and Barry Kaye Museum of Miniatures.

Furnishings From The Parlor

Frequently the parlor would contain at least one musical instrument, usually in the form of an upright piano or pump organ. Naturally in a grand house there may well be a music room but in simpler homes the parlor sufficed for such musical home entertaining.

Smaller homes would have upright pianos in their parlors. This miniature is handmade from wood.

Suitably styled for Victorian flamboyance, this harp and stool would be ideal for home entertainment.

A gilded harp of a classical design.

A clavichord of Victorian design.

A FAMILY ROOM

From the middle of the nineteenth century, street upon street of houses appeared on the outskirts of every major town in Britain. These homes were speculatively built, mainly for the lower middle classes, and almost invariably were similar in character inside too. Set around 1860 this front parlor in high Victorian style might be typical of any found in such a home. The rich red walls broken by the chair rails, the use of gold to highlight, and the dark floor and woodwork are important features of this room. Note too the presence of an upright piano, the green pot containing an aspidistra, and the mantel cover above the fire.

The room shown here has been decorated within an existing dollhouse. Cornices and a ceiling rose have been added to the ceiling and wooden board flooring sheet to the floor. Paint was applied not only to the ceiling and down to the picture rail level on the wall but also from the chair rail height down to the floor. The red flocked paper was then hung carefully between the bands of paint. Architraves, baseboard, picture and chair rails already stained were added after. Light fittings by Raymond Storey were fitted last.

When decorated, furnishing can begin. As a general rule, but particularly with a narrow room, it is advisable to start furnishing from the back. The curtains and pelmet were constructed first with the assistance of a miniature curtain-pleating device.

Natural fibers such as cotton or silk respond best in these because not every fabric takes up and maintains the shape impressed by the pleater. The use of hair spray is another hint worth considering. Also be prepared to pull and stretch the fabric in order to make the result look less rigid.

The same silk fabric was used on card forms to make the mantel cover and pelmet. Both these and the curtain edges were then trimmed with minute trim braid edging.

Two whatnots, laden with treasures, two work boxes, a center table, a plant stand, a fire screen, two chairs, and a piano furnish the room, while another carpet from MacDoc Designs graces the floor. The upholstered buttoned easy chair is in fact made of resin and skillfully painted to represent fabric. These chairs, along with an excellent sofa, are produced by John Hodgson and are available in unpainted form.

Ornaments and knickknacks are mostly of a simpler kind with items mass produced and not too costly. Among these here are the goldfish bowl and a bird in a cage.

ABOVE *The red-flocked wall covering and inexpensive objets d'art tell tale that this is the parlor of a less well-off English home. Note the bell pull, however, that suggests the existence of at least one live-in servant.*

1 Birds in cages gained in popularity; this miniature cage is handmade from brass.

2 No parlor would be complete without at least one whatnot or étagère. This one carries all the familiar trappings.

3 This whatnot is again laden with pictures, vases, enamel tray, and ornamental ceramic bust.

4 This miniature tiered cake stand is actually made of silver but the original might well have been finished in electro-silver plate. The delicious food is made by Miniature Dreams.

LEFT *A piano or other musical instrument was a familiar feature in parlors as this was a time before records, radio, or television, and people enjoyed entertaining at home. The door to this room is hung in an unconventional manner.*

❷ Extensively buttoned upholstery on curvaceous forms are typical of chairs from the late 1860s. Made by John Hodgson, this easy chair is cast from resin and its finish is painted.

❶ A collection of pinkish colored glass known as cranberry ware.

❸ An upright piano was a favorite piece of furniture for the parlor as it provided accompaniment for musical evenings. The seat of the stool lifts to reveal storage for music sheets.

TASTE AND DECORATION

China, glass and interior decoration were usually of poor quality in the more humble parlor and were frequently considered to be of questionable taste. Here furnishings are intended for show but budget has dictated less cost, quantity rather than quality being the rule of the day.

Tea and coffee sets were decorated in many ways but were never just plain white.

An assortment of decorative plates.

For use as table centerpieces or sideboard decoration the epergne came in many forms.

Pretty objects such as this were highly prized.

An array of foods for teatime.

Heavy decoration on equally heavy forms was a usual combination.

Glass was worked into many shapes but especially popular were fruit bowls.

Porcelain decorated with a blue and white oriental design became known as willow ware.

The Victorian love of nature manifested itself in many decorative objects.

THE DINING ROOM

Sited on the ground floor, adjacent to the kitchen, the dining room would be considered more masculine in style than the drawing room or parlor. Obviously still an important room in which to create the desired impression on one's guests, it conveyed feelings of security and solidarity. Walls covered with dark rich papers or deep wood paneling, ornate wood moldings, and substantial pieces of furniture were thought to create the desired effect. An imposing fireplace might dominate the room, the heat from which, unless screened, might prove too much for a dinner guest seated nearby. However, as a room used almost exclusively at night, it was required to look warm and sheltering and at its best when artificially lit by either gas or oil lamps.

Dado or wainscoting came into its own here, topped by a chair rail to protect the expensive wall coverings. Dining tables, often with extending leaves, between six and twelve chairs, and a sideboard came in matching sets although it was the latter that would be its owner's pride. Resplendent in ornamentation as well as in size, the sideboard was the embodiment of the room's main purpose. Displayed upon its generous top would be dishes and other accoutrements connected with the meal in progress, while vessels and containers of silver plate or porcelain not in immediate use filled the shelves that rose above. Drawers and cupboards beneath stored highly decorated plates and dishes, flatware, or linens together with other items related to the dining table. Naturally the best china would be used to impress important guests.

Further items of furniture might be armchairs, a sofa, plant stand, a secondary sideboard, glazed cabinets, and the now familiar array of smaller side or serving tables. Dark wood would usually be used for these pieces, with chair seats often covered with leather which was less likely to retain smells of food or smoke. While many dining-room window dressings were extremely ornate, simpler draperies or even shutters were sometimes favored, again in order to reduce the effect of lingering aromas. More busts and figurines, pots and jardinieres, small pictures, and table curios found space amongst the furnishings. Most popular as a table centerpiece was the tiered or branched epergne that cascaded with mildly scented flowers or a myriad of assorted fruits.

Pictures for the dining room were more or less obligatory. This time with themes of fruits, food, and flowers, together with all elements of hunting. Most pictorial outdoor scenes were considered suitable and frequently the actual stuffed and mounted heads of the unfortunate beasts themselves would grace the walls.

ABOVE *Plain chinaware for the dining room was completely unheard of. This table is laid for a simple family lunch.*

DINING ROOM FURNISHINGS

Solidarity was the key word for the dining room ambience and so naturally the most important pieces there should reflect that requirement. The sideboard or chiffonier was usually the most substantial piece having a large top, ornamental back and some form of display shelving. The dining table, too, would be equally impressive having a large solid top and sturdy legs and feet.

In keeping with Gothic and Elizabethan revival styles, this table has a rustic feel.

With heavy feet and a single supporting pillar, this table has the solidity that appealed to the Victorians.

Small cutlery cabinet doubling as a side table.

Splendid miniature chiffonier finished in suitable redwood.

A smaller folding table of mahogany. Note the tapered legs and casters which date its original at about 1860.

Interesting buffet or sideboard with center space and reflective glass.

A very robust, substantial sideboard intended to give a good impression.

DINING CHAIRS

As with many other Victorian furniture pieces, the chair appeared in a myriad of different forms. Here are just seven which reflect the contrast in styles.

Another variation of the balloon-backed chair from about 1850.

A combination of styles influenced the design of this chair.

The exaggerated arched forms of this chair are uncompromisingly Victorian Gothic revival.

While not epitomizing anything particularly Victorian, chairs of this type echoed the designs of previous styles. This bar-backed chair might be from about 1845.

An earlier form of the balloon-backed chair from about 1840.

Charles Rennie Mackintosh design of 1897.

The ornate back of this chair is in the style known as Belter.

This dining room, imaginably from a San Francisco painted lady of about 1893, also doubles as a parlor. A parlor pump organ is perfectly appropriate in such a room. From the 1860s to the 1880s the open fire began to lose favor in many American homes. Existing fireplaces would be blocked up and replaced with a new parlor stove. Made from cast iron in Albany, New York, in about 1865, the original of the stove here was dubbed "Eagle No. 2," being more ornate than many.

The main dining set of table, chairs, sideboard, and side table is in the comparatively less ornate Renaissance style, but the whatnot tiered display stand has all the shape and turnings in keeping with high Victorian. Decked out for a seasonal dinner the room contains Christmas items dating in style from the 1890s. Greetings cards, decorated plates, angels, trees, and candles give a festive touch to what otherwise might have been a fairly ordinary room.

2 *The sideboard in American Renaissance style also displays dishes.*

1 *The tiered étagère shows decorated Christmas plates, pictures, and an old spittoon to best advantage.*

THE DINING ROOM

ABOVE *This San Francisco dining room or parlor has been decorated with a collection of Christmas items.*

❸ *Small side or center tables were ever a favorite. Here Christmas items add to the collection in the room.*

VICTORIAN DINNERWARE

A good hostess would always use her most elegant dinner service when entertaining important guests. Plain white china was considered far too utilitarian for such occasions and so dinner pieces became available in a vast range of styles with intricate decoration.

A Royal Doulton pattern has been handpainted onto this miniature set.

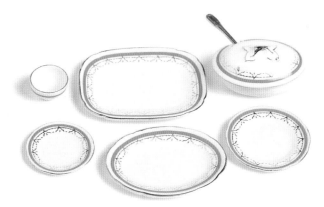

Examples from a set of tableware produced by miniaturist ceramic specialist Stokesay Ware.

A classic key pattern design produced by Stokesay Ware.

Three individual miniature pieces made of glass, porcelain, and silver.

A range of desserts typically found on a Victorian table.

Two British-made miniatures following Victorian examples.

VICTORIAN ECLECTICISM

This dining room might well be one found in a number of larger British town houses between 1860 and 1880. Then as now, not every home was constantly kept up to date because furniture and decoration was naturally intended to last for some time. In this room, for example, the chairs may have been made in the 1850s, the chiffonier in the 1870s and the fireplace in the 1880s, together producing another aspect of the Victorian look.

In addition, the dining, side, and window tables would all be revivals of their original styles. Dark wallpaper, rich woodwork, and substantial furniture draw the room together.

RIGHT *Mounted on the front of this dark fireplace is a brass bell used to summon the servants. Note the wooden mantel clock in curious Gothic style and the plaster epergne decorated with fruits.*

Paintings, ornaments, and decorative treatments are indications of a worthy Victorian dining room. The plaster epergne, complete with fruit, Gothic-style mantel clock, the stuffed elk's head, and bust of Victoria are significant touches that establish the room.

A room within another commercially made dollhouse was given a chimney breast with an opening cut in it to receive one of Trevor and Sue Cook's Victorian fireplaces. A complete ceiling piece was then glued into position with elaborate molding, also by the Cooks, mitered and fitted around its edges. All this, together with the top 2 inches of the walls, was then painted off-white.

OVERLEAF *The mood of this English dining room is masculine and somber, displaying an atmosphere of security and solidarity.*

❶ *No English home would have been complete without a bust of the beloved Queen.*

❸ *A crumb tray and brush were used for sweeping crumbs from the table.*

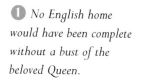

❷ *Chiffoniers would have been useful as a kind of second sideboard had it not been for the usual array of clutter.*

❹ *Fire irons in a stand ready by the fireside became known as companion sets.*

The preliminary painting, papering, lighting, and attaching of moldings was done in the manner previously described. The interesting task for the completion of this room was the construction and finishing of the furniture, all of which was made from miniature kits. The dining table, chairs, and sideboard all come together in a single set; the side table comes from another. Made from wood, each item can easily be assembled by following the kits' directions

LEFT *In this room, the original open fireplace has been boarded up and its hearth replaced by a cast-iron woodburning stove.*

carefully. The key to a successful piece is the attention given to the finishing. Good sandpapering and wood-staining are all-important, followed by a spray varnish of a satin finish for a more lifelike result.

The kits for the organ, stool, and whatnot are made by a different manufacturer and they are plastic. Having excellent detail, they are ideal for a project of this type. Certain wood stains work well on plastic too, and with a hint of a darker stain speedily wiped over a first stain of a paler color an authentic-looking patina can be achieved.

To complete the room, apart from the Christmas items, pictures, ornaments, and tableware have all been added. The beautiful glass decanter on the table contains real sherry for that extra touch of realism.

④ *The dining or parlor table shown without a cloth.*

① *An "Eagle No. 2" cast-iron stove that was set in front of the boarded-up fireplace.*

② *The family would gather around the pump organ in the parlor and, in this setting, sing favorite Christmas carols.*

③ *Another type of plant stand, holding a pot of Christmas poinsettia.*

ADDITIONAL SPLENDORS

As a further room used for the entertaining of often important guests, the dining room gave an added opportunity for show and display. In this room china- and glassware were used and many items were produced to enhance the process of eating and drinking.

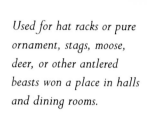

Used for hat racks or pure ornament, stags, moose, deer, or other antlered beasts won a place in halls and dining rooms.

To summon the genteel household to the meal table, gongs became most popular. This design would be from the late nineteenth century.

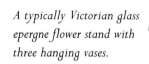

A miniature tantalus holding three glass decanters, 1898.

A typically Victorian glass epergne flower stand with three hanging vases.

This miniature is an exact copy of an original piece.

Glass decanter and wine glasses by Francis Whitemore.

A set of two glasses with decanter made of glass by Francis Whitemore.

Flooring, in the same sheet form as mentioned before, was laid next, followed by wallpaper, the fitting of the door unit, the baseboards, the chair rail, and finally the picture rails. To cut the baseboard and chair rail accurately by the fireplace, pencil lines were drawn on the wall to mark the fireplace's position. The 12-volt chandelier and candlesticks on the mantel were connected to the house lighting system by passing their wires through holes drilled through the ceiling and wall respectively.

The furniture for this room is all artisan-made with the exception of the chairs. These are in fact made from metal kits stained and sealed to look like wood and upholstered with cotton fabric.

Ready-made net curtains by Anne Ruff were complemented by drapes fashioned in a pleater but the pelmet is a reduced photocopy reproduction of a trompe l'oeil roller-printed valance designed by a James Burd of The Mount Zion Works, Radcliffe,

between 1825 and 1840. For the tablecloth a genuine late Victorian handkerchief was used, gathered at the back to avoid cutting and forced into shape with copious amounts of hair spray. The table underneath was protected from the spray by covering carefully with plastic food wrap.

The food by Miniature Dreams on both table and sideboard is evidence of a meal in progress. The comparatively simple rose bowl as a table centerpiece suggests this is an informal family gathering.

Ornaments and figurines cover every other surface whilst paintings of food and outdoor scenes decorate the walls. An indoor plant in a jardiniere, a bust of Queen Victoria on a pedestal, and an elk's head mounted on a shield have also found their homes here.

LEFT *In the window, the pelmet is of trompe l'oeil design that was roller-printed. The oils on the wall are originals painted by Tom Batt.*

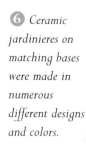

5 *The sideboard holds a meal's forthcoming delights. Nevertheless, an ornamental centerpiece would have been a permanent feature.*

9 *The seat of this chair would have been padded with horsehair.*

8 *A collection of items of a similar kind is always effective. These small figurines and tiny dwellings are all made of porcelain.*

6 *Ceramic jardinieres on matching bases were made in numerous different designs and colors.*

7 *Fresh flowers together with floral designs reflected the Victorians' great love of nature.*

5

6

7

8

9

THE STUDY

Apart from being the main retreat of gentlemen, much as the boudoir was for ladies, the study could also be a place where business and family accounts were settled. In this room there would be shelves of books, a handsome fireplace, comfortable chairs, and obviously a large desk. Frequently sited in what might previously have been the back parlor, the notion of a study or library increased in popularity as the prestige value of such a room became more and more appreciated. The distinction between library and study was less definable in smaller homes or suburban villas. Only larger mansions would be in a position to boast both.

The Gothic style was almost universally favored for this room. Not only did its dark solemnity seem appropriate but also its architectural style was well suited to built-in bookcases with traceried glass fronts and stained glass windows that curbed sunlight from damaging the books. Dark woods for furniture and woodwork of oak, mahogany, or black walnut would be set against walls of dark rich paper or wood paneling all contributing to the mood. Shelves might not necessarily be built in — matching freestanding ones served just as well. Neither were all bookshelves glazed, but tiny embossed leather valances added to the edge of each shelf helped to protect the books from dust and grime.

Besides bookshelves and an all-important desk, comfortable chairs with footstools, library steps, disguised safes, specimen chests, and drinks cabinets would be requisite furniture. A billiard table was a popular addition here, if a separate room was not available for this purpose. Apart from photographs in frames, busts, figurines, and reading lamps, other objects would reflect more masculine pursuits. Business papers, tobacco jars, decanters of port and brandy, trophies, maps, and globes spread themselves around the room.

Collections were highly prized; specimen coins, fossils, old hunting equipment, objets d'art, and antique curios were grouped in cabinets, laid out in special chests, or scattered liberally over tables. The study was also the ideal room for displaying the latest scientific toys. The magic lantern, the camera, the bioscope, the zoetrope, and the stereoscope were shown prominently giving rise to the supposition that this was the world of a man of many interests. Study use could take different forms and the owner of this room clearly uses it to paint.

Decorated in the fashion popular in the last quarter of the nineteenth century, the room might have been called "aesthetic." As an antidote to mass production, crafted items and natural materials were thought to be more individual. Unnecessary clutter and superficial decoration were treated with much disdain. The

collection of handpainted plates, simple bamboo
tables, and Chinese lidded pot is leaning towards
expressions of this thinking. The wallpaper is an
example of tripartite wall decoration, being frieze,
central field filling, and dado all in one. Originally
produced circa 1877 it epitomizes the decorative ideals
of the 1870s. That used in the miniature is another
photocopied reduction.

ABOVE *Described around the turn of the century as
"aesthetic," the style of this late Victorian room reflects the
tastes of the time. In sympathy with this Victorian thinking,
it is imagined that the room is occupied by an amateur
artist.*

FURNISHINGS IN A GENTLEMAN'S STUDY

Leather and dark woods with less intricate styling created the somber atmosphere of a more masculine room. Sensible pieces, chosen for very much function rather than decoration were deemed most suitable for a room that was solely dedicated to study and work.

Well-buttoned and upholstered Chesterfield sofa, ideal for the study.

This library chair from about 1830 metamorphoses into library steps when judicially unfolded.

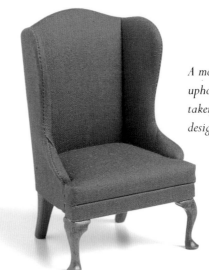

Buttoned leather-covered footstool, ideal beside a study fire.

A more rounded upholstered wing chair taken from an earlier design.

A very Victorian, mahogany-framed chaise longue suitable for study or boudoir. Possibly part of a set with other chairs, forming a parlor suite c.1870.

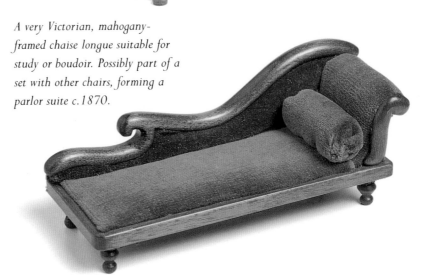

Although originating in the 1750s such chair design was popular well into the nineteenth century, particularly when upholstered in real leather as this miniature has been.

A Somber Retreat

The style chosen for this study is Gothic or, to be strictly accurate, Gothic revival. As mentioned earlier this style was much favored for libraries and studies. Here the two bookcases, fireplace, window, ceiling cornice, and fireplace mirror have columned cathedralic detail, while further Gothic elements are evident in the light fittings, black stained furniture, and fleur-de-lis-patterned wallpaper.

The serious purpose and function of the room is well defined by the presence of the huge carved table, serving as a desk, bedecked with instruments of work and study. Books on shelves, serious paintings, and the existence of a globe conform to the sobriety of the room. The only sense of light relief is supplied by the bright crimson-colored fabric that has been chosen for upholstery.

ABOVE *The nature of the pictures contributes to the sobriety of the room.*

1 *Two suitably masculine images in the form of bronze elephant and lion.*

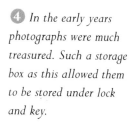

2 *A dark monk's cupboard, wrought iron candlestick, and mantel clock are all in Gothic vein.*

3 *Yet another form of stand, this time holding an urn.*

4 *In the early years photographs were much treasured. Such a storage box as this allowed them to be stored under lock and key.*

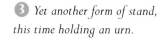

OVERLEAF *The theme chosen for the study is that of Victorian Gothic revival.*

❶ *A camera, stereoscope, and zoetrope were popular adult toys of the era.*

❷ *What might have been a dining table serves as a massive desk. The silver pen and ink stand, ivory magnifying glass, blotter, and photographs in frames add to the Victorian feel.*

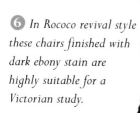

❻ *In Rococo revival style these chairs finished with dark ebony stain are highly suitable for a Victorian study.*

❸ *A most austere representation of Queen Victoria is in this dark marble bust.*

4 *Many types of creature were permanently preserved under glass domes. This handpainted miniature is possibly a chaffinch.*

5 *Celestial globes were in use as early as the seventh century, but by the end of the seventeenth century they were in a more recognizable form. For the Victorians the presence of a globe in one's home signified knowledge, education, and world travel.*

Although more classical in feel, this footstool blends in perfectly.

Library steps, whether practical or ornamental, suggested a notion that one was well read.

LEFT *The architectural detailing of the ceiling, cornice, and rose is truly Gothic. The small side window gives the study a monasterial feel.*

For the reproduction of the Gothic style, there are currently a number of miniature building components available, a few of which have been utilized in this room. From the Cooks come the heavy arched ceiling cornice and ceiling rose. After these were fitted to the room, the ceiling was painted off-white and slightly "aged" with cold black tea. The bookcase and fireplace, also from the Cooks, received a different treatment of paint effect to give the look of stone. These in turn were pushed into holes previously cut through the back wall.

The papering of the upper wall and dado was then completed in the normal way with the fitting of floor board sheeting, baseboard, and chair railing following suit. The pair of wall lights and matching chandelier by

lighting specialists Wood n' Wool were ideal for this setting and could be fitted in the usual way.

Conversely, the desk and five matching chairs were intended as a dining set and originally supplied in unfinished wood but, once given an ebony stain, they looked perfect for the room. The choice of drapes, rug, fire fender, and 'court cupboard' adapts readily to the style, forming a suitable background for the collection of interesting and decorative items. As now, room usage depended on the accommodation available. Clearly a larger house had more rooms which could be allocated for different purposes, such as a library, a billiard room, a smoking room, a music room, a ballroom, or even a private art gallery, each room being furnished in accordance with its function.

Where available space was limited, room usage obviously became interwoven. The drawing room, parlor, sitting room, study, and dining room might all be combined into one room, whereas a bedroom, bathroom, dressing room, and even nursery could similarly be merged. A typical Victorian example of this might be the rooms of the fictional detective, Sherlock Holmes. Here his study, library, laboratory, parlor, and sitting room are fused to create his main living area.

To the right of the room, there is a writing desk, beside which stands a bureau with library shelves above. On the left more shelves provide storage for a chemistry set, butterfly and bird's-egg collections, encyclopedias and additional books.

ABOVE *Leather wing chairs might normally be found in libraries and studies, and a central table surrounded by chairs might more conventionally be designed for dining room or parlor. Nevertheless, combined they furnish a study room ideal for a bachelor living alone, such as Sherlock Holmes.*

THE STUDY

STUDY PIECES

The accessories for the study were of sobriety. Designs would be simple and most often using dark woods and fabrics. Often, each piece had details to match the style of the room. Gothic revival was popular for the study and even clocks and letter racks of that design were available.

This small wine bottle holder can be carried from the wine store.

Three beautifully crafted miniatures made from silver.

A small tantalus of only two decanters.

Desk letter rack in vaguely Gothic style.

A beautiful miniature clock with wonderful Gothic styling.

A decorated letter rack.

Coal box with shovel that rests in a bracket on the back of the box. There is a tin lining located behind the lid, to hold the coal.

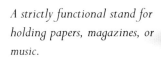

A strictly functional stand for holding papers, magazines, or music.

BOOKCASES AND SHELVES

Books on display gave the impression of their owner being well-read. Shelves of books could be purchased by the yard, such was the desire to create this illusion. As a result bookcases came in many forms; large versions built into the wall or free-standing ones that could be placed by a chair.

Large library bookcase with glazed portion below and embossed leather shelf trimmings to protect the tops of books from dust.

Tall library or study bookcase finished in mahogany stain.

Simple wall-hanging bookshelf complete with three small drawers.

Tall bookcase, American, from the late nineteenth century.

Simple four-shelved bookcase with useful drawer below.

COLLECTING AND DISPLAY

Prized book collections were often displayed behind glass and specimens of birds' eggs, butterflies and moths, stamps, coins or even rare tropical insects were arranged in shallow drawers. The Victorians loved collecting and showing off strange and wonderful objects from their travels.

This miniature contains books with leather bindings.

Glazed-top secretary bookcase. The top drawer opens down to form a writing desk.

Small side bookcase with two drawers for storage.

A very Victorian specimen chest. The Victorians loved to collect butterflies, insects, bird's eggs, and the like, and encase them in cabinets containing a series of small drawers.

Large study or library bookcase finished in mahogany.

STUDY DESKS

Often acting as a home office, the study's main requirement was a fairly plain but substantial desk; one that gave an air of responsibility and authority. Once again, desks came in a number of styles but the most popular ones were those based on well-established, traditional designs.

This kneehole desk has a board across the back.

Sometimes called a library desk, this one has a leather inset.

A Victorian walnut cylinder desk with small drawers, pigeonholes, and a pull-out adjustable writing slope.

Late nineteenth-century Carleton House desk finished to represent satin wood.

A little davenport in mahogany finish with drawers that pull out at the side, c. 1870.

Although not new in design kneehole, partner, and pedestal desks had their Victorian interpretations.

A MAN AND HIS TOYS

Essentially a masculine domain, the study contained, in addition to books and items of business, objects of a masculine choice. Collections and toys, and the latest scientific developments were possessions frequently found in a gentleman's study, and would be turned to for relaxation and amusement.

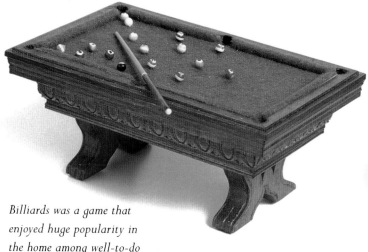

Billiards was a game that enjoyed huge popularity in the home among well-to-do Victorians.

The Victorians loved multipurpose furniture. The drawer of this little writing desk opens to reveal a lift-up bookstand.

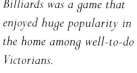

Penny slot machines were a novel source of amusement and were located in special galleries and on seaside piers.

Stereoscope complete with stand; a popular nineteenth-century toy.

A cylinder-type phonograph, the latest form of entertainment.

This miniature davenport has a leather writing slope.

Two boxed collection of butterflies and bird's eggs.

THE CONSERVATORY

Towards the end of the nineteenth century the conservatory was at the height of its popularity. Seen partially as an antidote to the gloom of the study or library, it often led off that room. Alternatively, a glimpse of greenery, if spied from the drawing room or parlor, appeared intriguing and so a conservatory might be sited to permit this.

The Victorians had an obsession with the romance of plants and nature, and no home was complete without flower arrangements and plants. The conservatory was not only practical for the cultivation of these for use in the rest of the house, but also offered the opportunity of experiencing a tropical environment first hand.

Usually tile-floored with part plain and stained glass paneled walls, the conservatory was furnished with a variety of wicker and bamboo pieces, cast-iron urns, and wrought-iron garden seats. Potted palms and colorful flowers, together with tropical plants and exotic birds in cages, created an original atmosphere of relaxation.

The use of stained glass was hugely popular with Victorians, initially because of its importance in the Gothic theme. By the 1880s to 1890s evidence of its use was everywhere. Sometimes forming detailed pictures or symmetrical designs, it decorated windows, doors, door side windows, and eventually the conservatory.

ABOVE *Although not quite Paxton's Crystal Palace, this miniature glasshouse is wonderfully elaborate. For this, its maker has used real glass and employed blue and green pieces in a most realistic way. Conservatories such as this might well have been freestanding, but more often they were attached directly to the house or linked by a short corridor of similar construction.*

Popularized by John Claudius Loudon, the conservatory caught the imagination of many who were in a position to have one built. The winter gardens of larger houses and European spas also stimulated the desire to have small versions added to even the more modest home.

With a greater availability of glass, now produced in larger sheets, conservatory and glasshouse specialists seized the opportunity to provide prefabricated models which they advertised in catalogs. This fairly modest example must have been typical of one sold in such a way.

ABOVE *Victorian Gothic in style, this conservatory would have been ideal for keeping plants alive and providing flowers for the drawing room or dining table all winter long.*

CONSERVATORY STYLE

Initially, cane or wicker furniture was considered only suitable for furnishing a conservatory but, as time went by, a wider range of furniture was made in this way. Nevertheless, along with cast iron most conservatory furniture was produced from these materials.

Cast-iron work in the form of a bench; however this miniature is resin.

Wickerwork was considered ideal for conservatory indoor–outdoor living.

This interesting miniature sofa is made from woven wire.

Cast-iron and wood constructed garden or park bench.

From about 1885, cast-iron rococo manifested itself in the form of this leaf design garden seat.

Designed for a conservatory or the porch, this two-seat sofa was made from fine woven cord.

INDOOR LIVING

When building his home, Glenmount, in Llewellyn Park, West Orange, New Jersey, Thomas Alva Edison incorporated all the latest trends. Designed by Henry Hudson Holly between 1880 and 1881 and built of brick, stone, and timber under a slate roof in popular "Queen Anne" style, an essential inclusion in the plan was a conservatory.

This conservatory (*right*) built in ½ scale is based on that very one. Originally, in the actual conservatory, the glass-paned panels that made up the greatest part of the walls could be removed in summer and replaced by screens of fine wire mesh. In the model the window panels are in place. The ceiling is of painted wood boarding and the floor has wood board also. All is painted a greenish white, giving a light, bright background to the plants.

Furniture of wicker, cane, and cast iron was considered suitable for furnishing an indoor–outdoor room of the time. The cast-iron table and chair set in the foreground in popular grape and leaf design would originally have dated from 1885, fitting into the category of rococo revival. Additional grape and vine decoration is found on various ceramic pieces, while a Chinese influence is evident too in the stone side table, garden seat, and matching pots. Naturally it is the plants that make this charming setting, for here palms, ferns, orchids, strawberries in pots, grape vine, parlor palms, and other plants conglomerate to create the ambience.

This room was built from scratch. On a foundation board measuring 18 x 15 inches, six 9-inch walls were formed: one plain, four with windows and the remainder with double-opening doors. A ceiling piece, already covered with strips of wood glued side by side, was then glued to the top of the walls. When set, the whole interior was painted white and subsequently given a wash of green. Finally, natural wood floors were laid down by the sheet and treated with a white wood stain.

To furnish, brackets were first fixed to the rear walls and window boxes containing flowers placed upon them. The largest palm took center stage with smaller plants placed around the walls. In true Victorian manner chairs, tables, and chaise longues were grouped together in small arrangements, offering quiet spots in which either to take tea or a solitary doze. The final addition was a number of birds. One of them is in a cage, but several others fly free.

❸ *Exotic plants flourished under glass.*

THE CONSERVATORY

❸

❹

❺

❶ *A firm-rooted Victorian design for cast iron was one that incorporated the organic forms of vine leaves and grapes.*

❺ *More Chinese influence is noticeable in this ceramic garden seat.*

ABOVE *A model conservatory based on that belonging to Thomas Edison in West Orange, New Jersey.*

❹ *Assorted pots and planters with organic decoration.*

❷ *A low cast-iron table matches the chair. The tea set is a copy of a Royal Doulton design.*

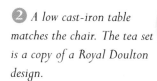

1 *At first considered suitable only for outdoor use, cane and wicker furniture found a place in the conservatory.*

2 *Classical forms were ideal for interpretation.*

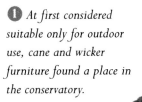

ABOVE *Small tête-à-tête areas were popular in nearly all rooms used for entertaining and the conservatory was no exception.*

THE CONSERVATORY

ABOVE *In readiness for someone to take an afternoon rest, this chaise longue is positioned under the palms.*

❶ *Grapevine decoration seems highly suitable on this jardiniere and stand.*

❷ *Orchids could be grown all year round in a glasshouse. These are in separate pots placed in a deep pewter planter.*

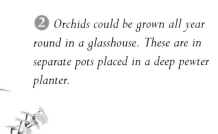

CONSERVATORY LIVING

Tea tables, plant stands, statuary and adequate seating were all important ingredients for furnishing a conservatory. The conservatory had to serve as a place to rest or to offer casual entertaining in addition to being used for the propagation of plants.

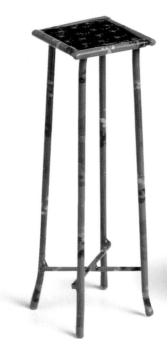

Bamboo and cane furniture were perfect for the conservatory and proved very popular.

A plant stand with cane or bamboo finish.

A further cast-iron piece, this time with a wooden top.

This miniature is finished to look like antique bronze.

Folding metal table of French design.

Folding wood and metal chair most popular in France.

Garden statuary was much favored as part of a romantic ideal.

FLOWERS, PLANTS AND BIRDS

The Victorians had a fascination with nature and tropical plants, and the conservatory offered a unique opportunity to experience them first hand.

Exotic birds gained popularity and were frequently housed in cages similar in design to conservatories. Oftentimes, birds would be encouraged to fly free.

Simple bird cage reminiscent of a design still used today.

Delicate bird cage on a stand mimicking the Crystal Palace.

Pretty white wicker plant stand. This miniature is handmade.

Elaborate cage in Victorian Gothic style.

An assortment of decorative miniature plants, designed especially for conservatory use.

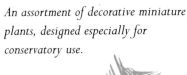

Handmade plant by Gillie Hinchcliffe.

THE MASTER BEDROOM

Although more subdued than first- or second-floor reception rooms, the Victorian bedroom was still furnished with a generous degree of taste, a sense of family and comfort. Very much a private room, significantly separated from those for public use by either stairs or passageways, a bedroom's look was a personal, individual one. With paler colors favored to give a lighter, brighter air, important criteria were cleanliness and hygiene. Again furnished with design origins firmly rooted in previous epochs, the room might still look out of date, as pieces of furniture from other rooms were frequently relegated there.

After 1840 matching bedroom suites came into vogue comprising the bed, armoire, dressing bureau, commode, and washstands; but even so, extra items found their way into the room. The bed could be anything from a four-poster in the 1840s, full- or half-canopied, wooden head- and tail-boarded, to the more hygienic brass or enamel being the most popular by the end of the century. All were highly decorative in ornamentation.

BELOW *Late nineteenth-century bed constructed of walnut and walnut burl.*

Where applicable, the armoire was the most important piece of furniture in the room. Usually mirrored, the facade could be double-, triple-, or quadruple-fronted with carved or molded features matching those found on the bed, commode, dressing bureau, and washstand. Of next importance was the washstand. Often fabric-draped or secreted behind a screen, it could be wide, having a marble or wooden top with perhaps a tiled splashboard, fairly narrow, with a shelf below, or just two-sided to fit a corner, but there was always space to hold a decorative washbowl together with its matching pitcher.

Depending on the room's size and the status of its occupant other furnishings were of an individual choice. By the middle of the nineteenth century it is probable that a dressing bureau was a standard feature in a larger bedroom with possible additions of a writing desk, chairs, footstools, an ottoman, wall shelves, a floor mirror, and a chaise longue. Built-in cozy corners of seating became popular alongside window seats or comfortable chairs being grouped around small, skirted tables.

OVERLEAF *The fabulously ornate dresser of this bedroom is in the Renaissance revival style and contains superbly fine details. The back measures 7½ inches high which, of course, means that full size it would be 7½ feet, looking more at home in a room with a very high ceiling. The bed too has a very high back, this one being made of walnut and walnut burl. This type of bed replaced the fully draped and canopied beds of the eighteenth and early nineteenth centuries. A bed of this kind of stature was particularly popular with new worldly men of business for adding that much required grandeur to the bedroom. Both miniature pieces are the work of Joseph Turner.*

BEDROOM FURNITURE

Washstands were a part of the bedroom scene quite some time before Victoria's reign. However, as with many other furniture pieces, styling changed to comply to the fashions of the day. Here miniature examples illustrate eight style variations.

A towel rail either side is the feature of this mahogany washstand. There is plenty of space on top for a pitcher, bowl, and other accoutrements.

Corner washstand with hole cut to accommodate pitcher and bowl.

A smaller and simpler version of the tile-backed washstand.

Plain, unadorned wood, a washstand of this kind could be found in a poorer home or servant's room. Note the hole cut in the top to hold the washbowl.

Fairly utilitarian corner washstands were usually constructed in classic designs.

Originally for garden, veranda, or balcony use only, popular Victorian wicker furniture eventually became used inside. A basic washstand with towel rail has been fashioned in wicker.

Marble-topped washstand with ceramic tiles for hygiene.

Marble-topped washstand with turned legs, small cupboard drawer, and tiled splashback.

BEDROOM DRESSING TABLES

The dressing table was a more recent invention and had a built-in mirror as part of the overall design. Varying in revival styles from Gothic to Renaissance and Classic to Belter these six dressing tables illustrate the interesting difference in styles.

The design of this English dressing table is influenced by classical style.

The Gothic forms of this dressing table team it with the rest of the matching set.

A vast dresser in Renaissance revival design. This miniature is an exact copy of an original.

With marble-topped surfaces and Renaissance revival decoration, this dresser has a matching armoire.

With a central full-length mirror, this design earns the name "dressing table."

Small dressing table finished in Belter style.

VICTORIAN BEDS

Once again beds varied enormously as the nineteenth century went by, starting with full- canopied beds of wood construction and ending with open beds made of brass and cast iron.

Tall, arched headboards and substantial footboards made important-looking beds.

This miniature brass bed is of the finest detail right down to its working casters.

A smaller version of a wooden head- and footboarded bed but nevertheless having detailed ornamentation.

This finely made chaise longue is equally suited for bedrooms, boudoirs, and dressing rooms.

Somber bedstead in Victorian Gothic style but in ebony wood finish.

With a frame made of wood, heavy drapes disguise this bed's construction. This tent style was still popular at the beginning of the period.

VICTORIAN BEDS

Whether having tall or short backs, or constructed of metal or wood, beds were always high in ornamental decoration, but essentially were built for maximum comfort.

Enameled metal-constructed bedstead in half-tester style.

A good substantial bed with detailed ornamentation.

Popular on both sides of the Atlantic in the 1800s was the making of patchwork quilts which incorporated irregular-shaped fabric scraps. This brass bed is adorned by a fine example.

Probably of Eastlake influence from the end of the nineteenth century, this comparatively simple bed has wooden head- and footboards of light walnut.

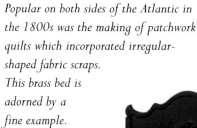

Mahogany wood-carved bed frame comparatively free of heavy ornamentation.

WARDROBES AND ARMOIRES

Usually massive and impressive, a Victorian wardrobe or armoire would dominate a bedroom since it was one of the most important furniture pieces found there. They often matched the bed, night table, dressing table and washstand having been purchased together as a set.

As part of a complete bedroom set, this armoire is again in Gothic form.

A simple pine cupboard with central opening door and drawer beneath.

A classically styled wardrobe or linen press.

"Hyde Park" armoire in good Victorian substantial style.

In Renaissance revival style, this armoire opens in three sections.

Although triple-fronted, only the mirrored door opens.

WASHSTANDS AND NIGHT TABLES

Before the advent of bathrooms and indoor toilets, chamber pots for nighttime use were hidden somewhere in the bedroom away from view. Many could be found under the bed but quite often pot cupboards were produced for keeping them out of the way and out of sight.

Small pot cupboard that in fact pulls the pot out on a drawer.

The top bar of this washstand is not so much a towel rack, but more a rail from which to hang fabric in order to protect the wallpaper behind from being stained by water splashes.

The door of this pot cupboard slides open from left to right.

Marble-topped washstand, typical of mass-produced furniture made from 1860 to 1870.

This bedside cupboard is part of a whole set designed in Gothic revival style.

Tall side table or pot cupboard in dark mahogany finish.

Two stone hot water bottles that fill from stoppers on the top.

GROOMING AND TOILETTE

Ladies' dressing tables could look most decorative, with matching sets made of glass, porcelain, papier mâché or silver, designed to hold items necessary for toilette. Often pitchers and bowls and lidded slop pails completed these sets although they would naturally be for use on the washstand.

Typical china dressing table of floral design, set with candlesticks, powder bowl, pin pot, and ring stand, all to be arranged on and around the matching china tray.

Tray, candlestick, and powder-bowl set showing, in addition, ornate sewing scissors and a set of tiny buttons.

From a gentleman's dresser this group includes a silver-backed brush, comb, shoehorn, and wig stand.

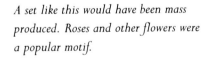

A pretty set manufactured in small English potteries after 1820, intended for working-class homes both at home and abroad. It displays a technique known as spongeware which was a cheaper form of decoration than expensive transfer printing.

This highly decorated matching pitcher and bowl also has a slop bucket and chamber pot to complete the set. The design of this miniature set is based on one in Queen Mary's doll's house.

A set like this would have been mass produced. Roses and other flowers were a popular motif.

Chinoiserie, alongside anything "oriental," was loved and interpreted in all kinds of ways. A design known as willow pattern was frequently used and here is a version on this pitcher and bowl.

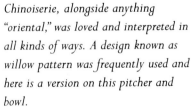

Functional white china pitcher and bowl set. Pictured too is a lidded slop bucket.

THE DESIRE FOR COMFORT

Marginally more comfortably furnished than its European cousins, this Victorian bedroom is perhaps typical of one to be found in a San Francisco Italianate villa of about 1882. British taste for bedrooms at that time was often less showy with a display of wealth and a high living standard reserved for more public rooms. The bed with matching table and commode here is in a high Victorian Renaissance revival style. In typical Victorian manner, where furniture and decoration take design themes from a range of influences, the bed set is mixed with other assorted pieces of Classical and Renaissance styles.

The love of oriental design, especially prevalent on America's west coast, is reflected in the intricate fretwork room-divider and lidded vase on a top shelf. The wallpaper, although American, has as its inspiration from the English cottage garden. The heaviest of the pictures are hung on chains from the picture rail in order to prevent damage to the wallpaper. Woodwork and furniture alike are of dark American walnut, while the drapes and bedspread are of a deep green, a most popular color at this time and one that has also been chosen for the glassware displayed on the shelves.

LEFT *A view into the bay window of the bedroom showing a small table of Eastlake influence together with a soft-seated side chair. The fretwork screen above is of an oriental taste.*

❹ *The bed, in high Victorian Renaissance revival style, takes center stage within the room. The sheets and pillows are English linen trimmed with lace and the cover is made from raw silk dyed a deep rich green.*

❸ *Based on a style of an earlier time this coffee set is of solid silver.*

❺ *A small corner washstand holds a decorative pitcher and bowl and a matching lidded chamber pot.*

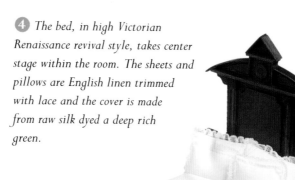

❻ *This needle-pointed footstool would probably have been worked by the occupant of the room. Home crafts were popular in the mid-nineteenth century.*

❶ *Fine handmade glassware in a typical Victorian green.*

❷ *Plant stands, étagères, small shelves, and other ornament holders were ever popular. In a simple pot this stand displays a type of fern.*

BEDROOM CHAIRS AND CHAISE LONGUES

Bedrooms were often used for more than just sleeping and were then furnished with comfortable chairs, dressing table stools and chaise longues. They could be used at any time of day, generally by the lady of the house, when the escape from a busy household was required.

A form of chaise longue with double armrests.

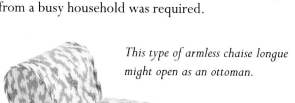

This type of armless chaise longue might open as an ottoman.

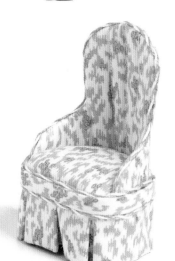

A simple bedroom chair upholstered in a pretty chintz.

Pretty spoon-backed chair upholstered with a floral print.

Frequently bedroom chairs were completely upholstered.

A curve-backed chaise longue with one extended arm.

Beautifully made miniature chair, following an 1850s style.

A further example of the varying balloon-backed chair.

GROOMING AND TOILETTE

Silver brushes, combs and mirrors (with bone or mother of pearl handles), and ceramic jugs and bowls with matching dressing table sets are all items reproduced by the modern miniature artisan.

All made from silver, the brush, mirror, and comb set has fine decoration.

Together with silver picture frames, lidded pot, and swan-necked scissors, the brush, comb, and mirror are all of mother-of-pearl.

Made mostly of silver these pieces are all handmade. The button hook has a shoehorn of mother-of-pearl and the tiny jewelry pieces have small diamonds.

An inexpensive set with a typical floral design.

Probably taken from a gentleman's washstand, this set includes a brass shaving mirror, shaving brush on a soap stand, and tiny toothbrushes.

A pretty pitcher and bowl set with handpainted Royal Doulton design.

An inexpensive little set with matching scent bottles.

These finely made wooden boxes contain firstly a razor set, each piece with a mother-of-pearl handle, and secondly a manicure set which includes two pairs of tiny scissors, a nail file, and nail polisher.

On the dark planked floor are large and medium-size rugs. There are odd chairs around the room and a trunk at the end of the bed to hold personal treasures belonging to the room's occupant.

This room has been created in another simple room box but this time an extension has been added to create a window bay. Floor, wallpaper, and wood moldings all have been worked in a manner previously described, with an extra ready-made fretwork piece added between architrave

PREVIOUS PAGE *The master bedroom is largely furnished with a matching set in Eastlake style.*

RIGHT *A close-up of the right-hand wall. The lamps beside the dressing-table mirror were probably oil-burning. However, electricity was widely used before the turn of the century; the light switch at the right of the door suggests that these lamps have been converted.*

moldings to form the bay window surround. The bed, dressing table, bedside chest, rocking chair, and lady's chair were all made from wood kits which were carefully sandpapered, stained, and satin-spray varnished. 12-volt light fittings for the ceiling, wall and beside the bed were connected to a copper-tape lighting system in the usual way. Beyond the window, a section of porch balustrade was positioned to give a dimension existing beyond the room. Pictures and ornaments were bought ready-made but a few good pieces like the silver coffee set help to make the room more outstanding.

⑦ *Designed to be sat in front of, the dressing table holds brush, hand mirror, jewel boxes, and a tray to catch hair pins and other small items of the toilette.*

⑧ *This chair, although in style, is of a poorer quality. After the Industrial Revolution mass-produced furniture became cheap and readily available.*

⑨ *Dressed in a lace cover the side table displays an array of family pictures. Victorians had a keen sense of family and with the advent of photography fancy frames containing family portraits became most popular.*

ABOVE *This English bedroom has been set in the early part of Queen Victoria's reign. Since it is not considered a public room, there is minimal ornamentation, with furniture in mostly classical revival style. Popular in the 1840s was the half-tester bed. Considered more healthy and hygienic than a bed with more drapery, its construction of brass or cast iron was equally cleanly. The hip bath and marble-topped washstand with a draped back, to protect the wallpaper, are definitely pre-bathroom whereas the love of decorative items, for example the encased fan displayed on the wall, was a trend that continued after the beginning of the next century.*

BELOW *The pierced gallery of this bedside pot cupboard forms a carry handle. The design is an interpretation of one from the reign of George III.*

ABOVE *Hip bath made from marble.*

Classic styled floor mirror, reinvented for the Victorian bedroom.

THE GENTLEMAN'S DRESSING ROOM

Although accessible from the upstairs hallway, the gentleman's dressing room was often adjoined to the master bedroom. Connected by an intercommunicating door, the key usually remained on the bedroom side letting a lady retain her privacy when required. It was quite normal for there to be a bed in the dressing room. This might be used on occasions when a gentleman returned late from his club, a business meeting, or a formal dinner when his wife did not accompany him, permitting him to retire without disturbing her.

Furnished fairly simply in a masculine style, a gentleman's dressing room was a private place where the only other person needing entrance was the valet. If not too small, the room might be used for writing short letters, an after-lunch nap or a quick drink before dinner after getting dressed.

A freestanding armoire or built-in closet was naturally the main feature of the room with perhaps a floor-standing dressing mirror, a comfortable chair, and facilities to wash and shave being of equal importance. Dark woods for all furniture pieces here would have been the most appropriate.

Wallpapers too would be of a darker tone with similarly masculine upholstery and drapes. For flooring, dark-stained boards or patterned parquet could have Turkish rugs partially covering them. Prior to the existence of a bathroom, this would be the room where a gentleman might bathe.

BELOW *This dressing room is in the American Renaissance style and of the 1880s. It is loosely based on that which existed in the residence of John D. Rockefeller Sr., at 4 West 54th Street, New York City. The furniture pieces have been made up from kits, stained, and then decorated with the use of stencils. The wallpaper and lamp fittings are very much in keeping with the original room.*

MASCULINE FURNITURE

A gentleman's dressing room might be furnished as reservedly as his study, with furniture pieces being more functional than decorative. The time spent here was primarily for dressing and resting either before or after a lengthy meal or function.

Classic five-drawer chest based on an eighteenth-century design.

Adjustable gout stool for use in conjunction with a chair or sofa.

Classic blanket box finished in mahogany.

This small silver-framed mirror and ceramic cream pot are the work of British craftsmen.

Again in classical revival style, floor-standing mirrors of this type found their way into many Victorian bedrooms.

A pretty side chair with some Gothic revival styling.

Being fairly plain this small chest of drawers is perfect for less important rooms.

MASCULINE INTERESTS

This dressing room might have belonged to an English gentleman who had obviously been a great campaigner. The traveling bath, elephant's foot, campaign chair, and military chests signify a lifetime spent abroad. Nevertheless, the choice of a William Morris wallpaper is clearly much nearer to home, with early portraits of Victoria and Albert indicating exactly where his loyalties lie. Other objects around the room are very much in a masculine taste. The bronze animals, hunting scene screen, pitchers, and drinking glasses emphasize this is a man's domain.

The freestanding wardrobe and military chests provide plenty of storage space for clothes. The detachable top section of the chest in the corner opens to reveal a writing desk containing several small compartments.

ABOVE *A ray of light from the window just catches the corner of the small military chest by the door.*

1 *The decoration of this screen relives one of the great Victorian outdoor activities.*

2 *Designed for military travel, this chest is of a design in use from 1800 until about 1870 and has protective brass corners and inset handles.*

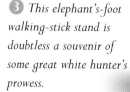

3 *This elephant's-foot walking-stick stand is doubtless a souvenir of some great white hunter's prowess.*

OVERLEAF *This gentleman's dressing room would be located on an upper floor in a large London house. Note the darker tones and masculine taste.*

This room measures 18 x 12 x 9½ inches high but has an internal wall of 5½ x 5 inches deep, to provide room for a water closet on the other side. Elaborate ceiling cornicing and a rose were glued to the ceiling before painting. Floorboard sheeting was used for the floor. The wallpaper is from a line of miniature ones and is taken from the original William Morris "Strawberry Thief" design first printed in 1883. The door, baseboard, and picture rail were stained a deep rich mahogany, a wood finish extremely popular throughout the Victorian age.

For furnishing, almost every item was bought ready-made at either fairs or a miniature store. The bed, wardrobe, bedside cabinet, campaign chair, and military chests are all by Escutcheon and made in Britain. British too are the wallpaper, ceiling cornice and rose, light fixtures, bronze pieces, and the fireplace. The pictures of Victoria and Albert in their early years and the tin traveling bath were specially commissioned. The screen with hunting scenes is by Natasha, and the drapes and cornice are both from Anne Ruff.

The detail of the bed's legs and bulbous turnings are true Victorian.

❶ *The design of this fireplace would be about 1850. It is made by miniature specialists Sussex Crafts.*

This folding campaign chair is originally of an eighteenth-century Dutch design but versions of its kind fitted well with Victorian interiors.

Although fundamentally of a design from the late eighteenth century, armoires of this type were popular until the 1850s.

A tin traveling bath. The straps unbuckled to release the lid.

The form of this chair dates from a much earlier date but, reshaped as one of many revival styles, it resurfaced as Victorian.

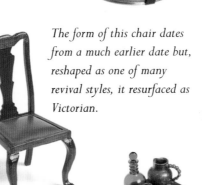

❷ *This table holds a small dressing mirror, probably used for shaving, together with moustache curling irons, and a gentleman's watch and chain.*

Souvenirs from foreign places were considered most desirable. This table is clearly of an Eastern flavor.

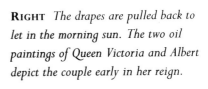

RIGHT *The drapes are pulled back to let in the morning sun. The two oil paintings of Queen Victoria and Albert depict the couple early in her reign.*

THE LADY'S BOUDOIR

This is not quite the soft, lacy, pink lair of the femme fatale that perhaps the modern interpretation of "a lady's boudoir" might imply. However, this was a private room to which a lady, and perhaps a few intimate friends, might retire. Here she could indulge in feminine pursuits: drawing and painting, writing poetry or letters to friends, embroidery and sewing, reading romantic novels, or engaging in hobby pastimes and crafts. Where a separate sewing room did not exist, a corner for dress- and curtain-making would be found with a new model sewing machine taking pride of place. This was a corner of the house which was exclusively hers.

Decoration leaned toward the romantic with objects chosen in strictly feminine taste. Collections of scent bottles, paperweights, small figurines, silver table sets, and covered boxes containing ribbon-bound letters would be displayed here. Naturally colors were light and pretty with floral designs for drapes and upholstery favored.

Furniture again could vary. Soft upholstered chairs, small sofas, or a chaise longue would be grouped for conversation or private relaxation. Footstools, workboxes, display cabinets, wall shelves, a small desk, the usual small tables, and perhaps a set of dressing table, bed, and armoire would be arranged to fill the room. A fashionable idea of the late 1880s was to prop a painting on an easel artistically draped with fabric or a shawl.

Pictures of a romantic, sentimental nature hung from the walls while country themes of sheep and shepherdesses took the form of figurines.

RIGHT *Many ceilings were highly ornamental.*

❶ *A beautiful flower arrangement by Flowers 'n' Things. The two shoe ornaments were considered slightly saucy.*

FEMININE FLAIR

The general arrangement of this room may seem one of complete disorder, with different styles of furniture and differing patterns used together for the wallpaper, rug, and screen, but for a fashionable New York private room of the 1880s this was just the look desired. Even furniture and drapery coordinated by the use of the same plain colored fabric would have been judged too tame for many tastes, whereas the ornamented ceiling with highly decorative cornicing around, swathed drapery, and embellishing fretwork would be considered very fashionable.

Nevertheless, this is a lady's inner sanctum, her private boudoir, a place where she might surround herself with the things that please her. The collage screen, the painting on the easel, the writing desk, and open scrapbook are evidence of her interests. The room also contains a dressing table, armoire, and bed, providing the facilities of a dressing room, and the presence of a chaise longue, chairs, and stools enable the entertaining of intimate friends.

RIGHT *A view through into the bed alcove on the right-hand side of the room.*

① *Both screens and paper scrap work were essentially Victorian; here the two combine.*

② *The cutting and pasting of scraps and other paper souvenirs was a popular pastime.*

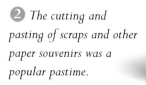

❸ *A single-door armoire in typical Victorian style.*

The carpet bag was an essential Victorian holdall.

❸

A ladies' dressing table might well be found within the boudoir.

This floral decoration has been made from shells.

OVERLEAF *A lady's boudoir of decidedly feminine taste furnished generously and appropriately to suit this most private place.*

① Reproductions of classical design were readily available. Produced in brass, this one is of the Roman god, Mercury.

ABOVE *A corner of the boudoir showing the writing desk.*

③ The draping of an oil painting positioned on an easel was thought most artistic.

② This ladies' writing table provides one of the basic requirements of the room.

Ornaments for the boudoir would have been essentially feminine, like these two small figurines.

④ The lady whose room this might be would probably have worked this stool cover herself.

A separate room box was made to accommodate this room and for furnishings a number of approaches were combined. Firstly, the ornate ceiling piece and cornices were purchased ready-made, each being trimmed and fixed to the ceiling as a whole and painted when in place. Secondly, the floor of parquet blocks was made up by joining a number of ready-made sheets, with sandpapering and polishing thereafter. Thirdly, the papering and fixing of wood moldings were carried out in the usual way.

Now the room was ready to furnish and for this a number of inexpensive imported pieces were used. Today there is a good quantity of well-designed, cheaper furniture available. It is usually the excessively thick varnish and unfortunate staining that let them down. However, with considerable sandpapering, perhaps slight remodeling with an electric tool and knife, and restaining, quite pleasing results can be achieved.

Nearly all the furniture in this room was subjected to this treatment and with new upholstery the items appear unique. The screen, previously of fabric, was given new panels of miniature scraps and cheaper picture frames received prints of an appropriate nature. Finally a few bought items of silver, bronze, china, and glass, together with a commissioned floral arrangement from Flowers 'n Things, contributed to the authenticity of the room.

BELOW *This is possibly a boudoir or sewing room adjoining a private sitting room. Here a dressmaker's dummy and sewing machine are positioned in the window for good light. In addition the owner of this room has shelves of collected knickknacks, a curio cabinet in which she displays glass paperweights, and an interesting teapoy. Made from mahogany, this early Victorian sarcophagus-shaped teapoy has a top that lifts open to reveal jars and bowls for the blending of teas. The omnipresent center table in the Renaissance revival style mirrors the taste of Europe and was popular from the late 1850s until the 1870s. Here it is doubling as a work table. Note the ceramic footbath decorated with pretty floral design.*

FURNISHINGS FROM THE BOUDOIR

Boudoir furniture should be decorative, as well as being functional, with sewing tables and small chairs that are pleasing to the feminine eye and where friends could be entertained in comfort.

This lady's chair has a carved back that runs into the arms but is mounted on Queen-Anne-style legs.

Bentwood chairs came in a number of different forms. This rocker might be from the 1850s.

Victorian-style chair. This miniature is upholstered with antique silk.

A form of nursing chair might be suitable for the boudoir.

Small black lacquer lady's writing desk with handpainted decoration.

This elaborate workbox has been handcrafted from fine wicker.

Religion was an important part of Victorian life and many people created private chapels or had small alter tables.

From about 1840 teapoys were used to store different blends of tea. Today many have been turned into sewing boxes.

Sometimes, home craftwork incorporated dried flowers as materials. This fire screen is decorated in such a way.

A LADY'S PASTIMES

Since the boudoir was probably the room in which a lady would pursue her crafts and pastimes, a sewing machine, sewing basket or artist's easel might well be found there alongside finished pieces of her work. Needlepointed screens, seashell or papier mâché craftworks, along with scrap books and amateur paintings are just some of the items that would decorate the room.

A Singer treadle sewing machine of an early style.

This treadle machine could fold down out of sight within the wooden case.

Under the influence of earlier designs this workbox in revival style has an outdoor scene painted on its lid.

A more functional artist's easel of a type recognizable today.

Stained glass came into the fore in many Victorian homes. Here colored glass has been incorporated into a screen.

Pictures resting on easels became the vogue. This easel has built-in illumination.

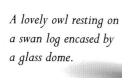

A lovely owl resting on a swan log encased by a glass dome.

Stuffed birds and other creatures appeared frequently in Victorian homes.

When leather luggage could not be afforded, these carpet bags offered a good substitute.

THE NURSERY

ocated on an upper floor or even in an attic room, nurseries were required to be more functional than decorative. Therefore, compared to reception rooms and adult bedrooms, they were relatively plain. However, by 1870 wallpapers were specifically designed for the nursery and, for use in conjunction with these, came friezes, usually having an educational theme.

Depending on the size of the house, nursery quarters might comprise a night nursery for sleeping and a day nursery for learning and recreational pursuits. In very large houses, accommodation for a nurse or governess would be located in an adjacent room.

Decoration would be light and consideration would be given toward keeping the room clean. Furniture too would be light or painted without much ornamentation, function being more important than giving pleasure to the eye. Closets and shelf space were required here for the storage of toys, books, and learning materials as by day the room doubled as a schoolroom.

ABOVE *The corner of this British nursery is very prettily decorated. The semicircular form at the head of the register grate in the fireplace would date the room from around 1830 to 1850, as would the half-tester child's bed of brass and steel. The little doll's house is possibly later but it would be likely that a nursery would remain largely unchanged for many years.*

NURSERY FURNITURE

Nurseries were seldom over-decorated or elaborate. The emphasis was on cleanliness and safety. Cribs and childrens' beds were frequently made of brass or cast iron, usually with high sides to prevent a toddler falling out. Simple furnishings and bare wooden floors were often the norm.

Wicker became acceptable in nurseries too, particularly in the United States.

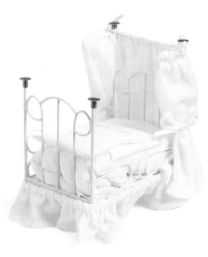

Half-tester-style child's bed constructed of steel and brass.

Metal-constructed baby beds were considered both safe and hygienic.

School desk with its own seat attached, often used in private schoolrooms.

For both child and adult use, this is an early form of stroller.

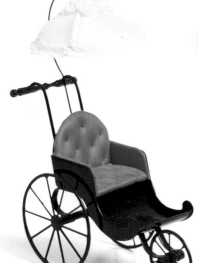

School desks of this design were of necessity assembled in rows.

Tall nursery fender of brass and steel. Towels could be hung to dry over its brass top rail in front of the fire.

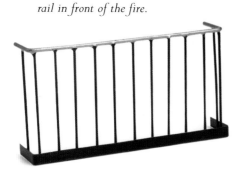

Child's pram beautifully made in miniature from metal and real leather.

NURSERY TOYS

By the end of the nineteenth century all manner of childrens' toys had been developed as a result of current thinking that encouraged education through play. Toy forts, model kitchens, dolls, Noah's arks, rocking horses and of course the dollhouse were amongst the favored toys of the day.

A miniature toy town set made of card as a copy of one made by the McLaughlin Company and entitled "Pretty Village."

A fort was a typical late Victorian toy.

A form of spinning circus toy.

A miniature bandstand

A small shop toy, as yet unfilled and a little cardboard puppet theater.

Plain wood miniature dollhouse made in late Victorian style.

By the turn of the century no self-respecting nursery was complete without some form of rocking horse.

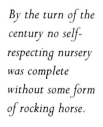

CLEANLINESS AS A PRIORITY

Following the edicts that prevailed, this nursery might have existed anywhere. Set towards the end of the nineteenth century, it may have been of a more charming appearance than many. The easy-to-sweep floor, simple functional furniture, sensible lighting, and high nursery fender all denoted the room's main purpose. The wallpaper frieze of Kate Greenaway design, nursery pictures of children playing, and furniture for storage are all typical of late Victorian nursery styles. Window seats of different types were now immensely popular and here one has been built into the bay window, an ideal spot for listening to a story read by nanny. Toys, a table for study and play, and a washstand are important features of this room.

ABOVE *Window seats became a vogue but this one is used for storytelling.*

① *A rocking horse was a classic nursery toy. This miniature by Sue Austen is a copy of one made by Lines Brothers after the turn of the century.*

② *A beautiful chair of classic design by craftsman David Booth.*

③ *What could be more classic than a prettily dressed child's doll?*

④ *Assorted toys and games including a cup and ball, and diabolo.*

④

⑤

⑥

⑦

⑦ *High nursery fenders with a towel rail combined practicality with child safety.*

⑥ *This box contains reading cards under the title "Morals for Children."*

ABOVE *As a child's domain, the nursery is a bedroom, playroom, sickroom, and schoolroom combined in one.*

⑤ *Based on the early Dutch kitchen, this model was both educational and a plaything.*

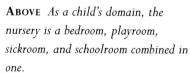

Again set within a dollhouse, this room was not hard to put together. The door, ceiling cornice, picture rail, and baseboard are all simple in design and just spray-painted an antique off-white. The wallpaper comes printed with its frieze and is widely available from good miniature stores. The floor is sheeting, this time of fiberglass construction from Reuben Burrows. Furniture of plain white wood was spray-painted to match the woodwork and other ready-made pieces were left in their already finished state. The drapes and window cornice were adapted from those by Anne Ruff, with extra fabric used to form the window seat by covering padded pieces of card.

To complete the room, classic toys such as a doll, dollhouse, and Noah's ark were chosen as those most likely to be found in a nursery of the more prosperous Victorian home.

❶ *The essential items of the washstand are included in this pretty set of pitcher, bowl, beaker, and chamber pot. The brass kettle is for carrying hot water.*

❸ *A well-constructed Victorian nursery plaything, the dollhouse.*

❷ *This child's bed is of a simple Victorian design.*

LEFT *A washstand in the nursery often proved very useful.*

THE BATHROOM

For early middle-class Victorians the practice of washing and bathing in the bedroom or dressing room was an accepted one. The washstand with its pitcher and bowl was a permanent feature in the room but a bathtub or hip bath made of zinc or copper had to be brought in each time bathing was required. Placed on a bath blanket, with oilcloth spread out below, the tub would be filled with hot water hand-carried from downstairs.

With the advent of indoor plumbing in the last quarter of the nineteenth century, washstands could be given faucets and permanently fixed bowls with plug holes and piping for the waste water. As for bathtubs, these now needed a permanent fixed site. Early bathrooms were converted from dressing rooms and secondary bedrooms and were therefore comparatively large. Here bathtubs could be permanently plumbed in with washbasins alongside them. Early fixtures were boxed within cabinets and varying encasements in an attempt to disguise their real function.

By 1880 water closets joined the bathroom scene and were similarly disguised, but a certain anxiety about their being inside the house at all resulted in them being sectioned off within a separate cubicle. The decoration and internal construction of the dressing room or bedroom remained within the now-converted bathroom and it was the style of these former rooms that represented the bathroom look for many years. Other bedroom furniture, such as armoires, dressers, side tables, and even sofas, followed the washstand into the new room, compounding the bedroom mood.

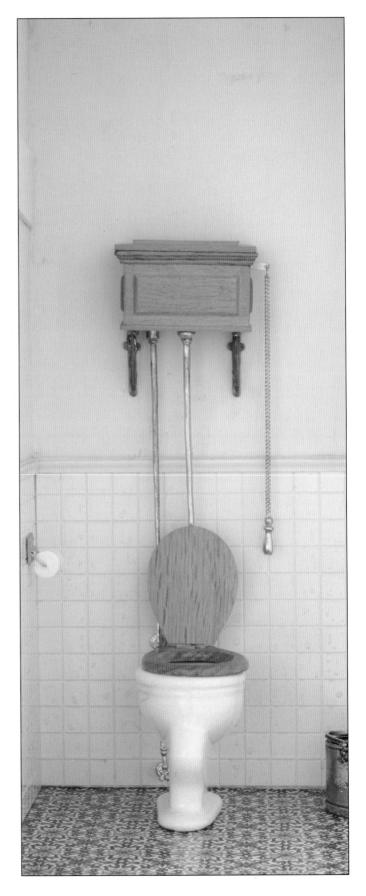

RIGHT *Water closets were usually separate from the main bathrooms and frequently located at the back of the house on the ground floor. This one has a typical wood-encased cistern on cast-iron brackets with matching seat and cover. Half-tiled walls and a linoleum-covered floor are further typical features.*

When established fresh pride and consideration was given to the bathroom. Towards the end of the century thought for hygiene plus a familiarity with the room led to the demise of boxed-in fittings and even washstands, producing individual roll-topped baths of vitreous enameled cast iron with ball and claw feet, the pedestal washbasin, and toilet bowls decorated with either raised scroll work or floral design decals or transfers applied both inside and out. A water tank mounted on metal wall brackets was fixed high above the bowl while the lavatory seat was made from varying types of wood. Although plumbing and the gas geyser were available from the 1860s, before 1850 washstands, outhouses, and chamber pots were commonplace. Even by the 1890s, indoor bathrooms were by no means standard, particularly among the less well-to-do.

ABOVE *The wooden boxed-in bath and washbasin with marble top and splashback are in the style of earlier bathroom fittings. Perhaps of greater interest in this room, however, is the ceiling, which would have been made of tin. Introduced in the late 1880s, ceilings of pressed tin were initially intended as prefabricated substitutes for the then fashionable carved and cast plaster ceilings, which were high in decoration. However, they found immense popularity in their own right. Ideally suited for small rooms where humidity was a problem, their application in bathrooms, kitchens, and sculleries was far better than any ceiling made of plaster.*

BATHING IN LUXURY

The bath, washbasin, and water closet with wooden seat and wood-encased tank above are typical fittings for a Victorian bathroom of about the 1880s. Also, in accordance with the nature of this new room, the corner whatnot and decorative plant stand look as though they have been "borrowed" from elsewhere. The colors used, the size, and the decorative treatment are indicative of the era.

A special touch is an addition of a cast-iron radiator, indicating the luxury of hot water being pumped from a boiler located on a floor below. Usually finished to represent wood or tiles in geometric patterns, linoleum was a Victorian invention. This bathroom boasts what would then have been the latest in floor coverings.

Housed in a tiny room box, the decoration in this bathroom was carried out in the conventional way but with the ceiling paint brought about 2 inches down the walls; a prestained cornice was fixed between the walls and ceiling after the paint was dry. As with both the hall and parlor explained earlier in this book, wallpapering was done in top and bottom halves with the chair rail glued over where the two papers met.

The bath set is another kit sprayed with an excellent kitchen appliance enamel spray, with tank, cabinet, and lavatory seat stained with a two-part wood stain. When all the fixtures and fittings were glued in place, a few accessories brought the room to life.

RIGHT *The Victorian bathroom was usually converted from a dressing room or small bedroom and therefore retained many of the room's original features.*

As a new concept developing in an industrial age, manufacturers were keen to produce bathtubs in a wide range of designs. Curiously they have altered little in shape from the tubs in use today. Note the portable tin bath (bottom left) of a kind still used in most homes at the turn of the century.

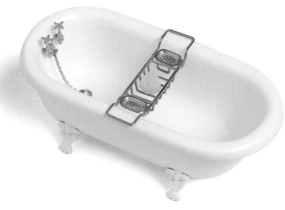

Standard bathtub on feet but note the "bottle" side-mounted faucets.

Boxed-in bathtub being one of the earlier forms of fitting.

Bath with brass mixer faucet and shower spray attachment.

Deep roll-topped bathtub standing on four feet. Note the detail of the plug.

Galvanized steel portable bathtub, used in poorer homes. This miniature is made from resin.

Bathtub of a roll-top design with external decoration.

THE INDOOR WATER CLOSET

By the last quarter of the century the water closet moved with trepidation into the house but still remained in a separate compartment away from the rest of the bathroom. Initially encased within wooden boxes, ceramic toilet bowls were later developed in a highly decorative, ornamental style of their own right, quite often matching the decorative style of the wash basin.

Small commode chair with bowl inside a cupboard.

"Thunder Box" water closet of an early Victorian design.

Early wood-enclosed lavatory bowl with tank above similarly encased.

Ceramic bowl with overhead tank together with authentic-looking wooden seat.

Simply shaped bowl connected to an overhead cistern.

ABOVE *A roll-topped bath standing on four feet permitted cleaning underneath.*

LEFT *Towards the end of the century many homes could boast a form of central heating. The radiator here is of an early design.*

THE KITCHEN

Whether positioned on the main floor or in a basement below, the kitchen was essentially a place of work. Plain off-white walls and a well-scrubbed floor dictated the overall look of the room. This was the domain of servants and therefore decoration or ornamentation was completely inappropriate here. A scullery for household chores and pantries for the storage of china, equipment, and foods all led off the kitchen and away from the main reception rooms.

Nevertheless by the 1870s some changes had occurred. Now, more often than not, the kitchen was on the main floor but as far to the back of the house a possible. The introduction of gas supplies and certain hygiene measures encouraged new thinking about this long-neglected area and, in America particularly, consideration was given towards those who worked there. With a decreasing number of staff, the lady of the house might spend more time in the kitchen herself, often completing more important aspects of the cooking.

Ease of cleanliness, efficiency, and a certain cheerfulness became all-important factors. Walls were painted in neutral colors of beige, cream, or gray. Sometimes wallpaper might be hung and subsequently varnished in order to be cleaned easily. Floors were often of oiled and varnished hardwood with a hard base inset for the stove. Rag rugs, carpet pieces, or decorated oilcloths might soften the appearance. The advent of linoleum was well received as it was even easier to clean.

The 1850s brought new ornamented cast-iron stoves with bright nickel-plated decoration. Wooden iceboxes housing blocks of ice were now more efficient, with the ice at the top letting air flow around it. Pie safes were still popular, with glazed-fronted cabinets displaying china a favorite for kitchens. A light and airy atmosphere was the mood for the kitchen, with furniture comprising a main central table, which must have an easily cleaned surface, a plumbed-in sink, a reliable stove, side tables to facilitate work routines, and adequate dresser space to insure maximum efficiency. Essential items were pastry board and cutters, a rolling pin, mincing or grinding machine, scales, iron or copper pots, kettles, knives and choppers, and the latest item, the jelly mold. The kitchen range was also updated, offering more decorative styling and time-saving features. Water was now brought direct to the sink either using a pump as in rural areas, or through a faucet mounted above the sink which was attached then to a whole plumbing system.

ABOVE *This large English kitchen is typical of one which might be found in a basement of a great English house, where many kitchen staff would ensure its smooth running. Created by John Hodgson, this model is now part of the Guthrie Museum on view at Hever Castle.*

KITCHEN IMPROVEMENTS

The aftermath of the American Civil War brought more rapid changes in the American kitchen than those experienced in English homes. The same advancements did not occur in Britain until after World War One. In both cases, however, the dwindling number of kitchen staff drove the housewife into the kitchen. Steps towards comfortable surroundings and greater efficiency now became the housewife's concern.

This American kitchen of the late 1890s shows the early signs of a style we recognize today. Kitchens became a more hospitable place. There is a new sweep-clean floor, chinaware displayed on shelves, and cooking items stored within easy reach.

RIGHT *Decoration in the kitchen was minimal. Note the dado of wooden planking.*

The china closet and dresser contain shelves as well as plenty of drawers, giving accessible storage for items in regular use. Shallow open shelves were recommended for the storage of household products, making them easy to find and also providing a decorative display. The work table still stands in the center of the room but now has drawers containing the necessary tools for different jobs.

OVERLEAF *Set after the American Civil War, this bright looking kitchen is one designed for cleanliness and efficiency.*

❶ *China closets had enclosed storage below while more decorative items could be viewed through glass doors on the shelves above.*

❷ *Pans of different sizes were made of cast iron. These miniatures are not heavy, but full-sized they certainly would be.*

❸ *Ornate cast-iron stoves of this type stood on sheet metal stove boards. There are removable hot plates and trivets to heat irons.*

❹ *Ice is stored in the compartment above, keeping food cold on the shelves below.*

BATHROOM EQUIPMENT

Wash basins shed their initial wooden shrouds and developed into the pedestal-type we recognise today. Decorations of flowers, leaves and plants appeared on toilet bowls, wash basins and other bathroom chinaware which became as pretty as the pitcher, bowl and pot sets they began to replace.

Pedestal hand basin complete with faucets, plug, and drain hole.

Enclosed washbasin under "marble" top and splashback.

Ceramic lavatory bowl with typical floral decoration.

Early radiators were not so streamlined.

Heating geyser fueled by gas.

Brass towel rail for the bathroom.

This early bidet bowl should be set within a wooden case.

A ceramic footbath that matches the bidet.

❺

❻

❼

KITCHEN FURNITURE

Easy-to-run and easy-to-maintain were the themes that dictated the look of the late-nineteenth century kitchen. Tables had drawers in which to keep knives. Food and cooking equipment were stored in cupboards within easy reach; with fewer servants to help, efficiency was the key.

Pine-finished table with a drawer positioned in the side.

Drop leaf kitchen table with painted legs but plain pine top.

Simple single-drawer table made in pine.

Mesh-fronted and -sided meat store that would have been located in a cool place or even outside.

Kitchen or pantry storage cupboard finished in stained wood.

Small labeled spice cabinet, designed to hang on the wall.

Expanding clothes drier that would stand in front of a fire or kitchen stove.

Simple clothes drier made of wood.

THE NEW KITCHEN

Having remained largely unchanged for hundreds of years, the kitchen sink was adapted to become an integral part of the evolving kitchen.

Draining boards and faucets with running hot and cold water were fitted to sinks along with fixed or tiled splash backs that were easier to keep clean.

Complete sink, draining board, and copper geyser from the late nineteenth century.

This dry sink with shelves above the splashback replicates kitchen furnishings found in the 1869 home of Harriet Beecher Stowe in West Hartford, Connecticut. Miss Stowe, together with her sister Katherine, regularly wrote articles describing the contents of a "proper Victorian home" for the American Woman's Home *magazine. Her kitchen had shelves all around the walls.*

An alternative style of sink with drainer.

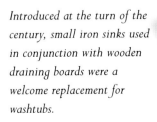

Introduced at the turn of the century, small iron sinks used in conjunction with wooden draining boards were a welcome replacement for washtubs.

Typical British ceramic sink, standing on brick piers.

An icebox stands on the kitchen floor, keeping food fresh and away from dust and dirt. The cooking stove too has an opening beneath it, permitting easy cleaning. Fresh water comes directly to the sink, this time via a pump, but faucets were installed before the end of the Victorian period.

Walls and ceilings are finished in off-white and the woodwork of the door, dresser, china closet, and wainscoting are painted similarly. The tin top of the table was a forerunner to enamel, which in turn was to be replaced by plastic. The emphasis was on cleanliness and hygiene, and as a result forms are comparatively plain and easy to keep clean.

To achieve a unifying look in the room, more furniture kits were made up. Each was then finished with the same spray paint. The table, dresser, and china closet are by B. H. Miniatures. Selected for their fine detail, the appliances are Chrysonbon; although

made of plastic, their scale is perfect. The cooking stove stands on its own "etched metal" base intended to keep heat and coal dust away from the floor. It has pots and lids that open and swivel trivets for hot irons. With careful painting of the components during assembly, the finish can be made to look exactly like cast iron. The icebox too has doors that open, internal shelves, water drip-pan and even a block of "ice." The dry sink, pump, towel bar, and shelf equally have fine-scale finish.

Accessories, as usual, complete the room. Dishes are placed in the china closet, plates, groceries, cooking utensils, coffee grinder, and other kitchen equipment fill the dresser, and pie-making is in progress on the kitchen table, where there is also a beautiful basket of fruit.

LEFT *An old kitchen broomstick left by the door, ready to make sure that the floor was always kept clean.*

Little drawers for storing spices were an early idea.

5 *This dresser has capacity for storage and the display. Of interest is the bottom board for keeping larger items.*

7 *New coverings on the work table were easier to keep clean. Here pies are in the making but note the beautiful basket of fruit.*

6 *The dry sink has a water pump on one side and a separate bowl for the water.*

KITCHEN EQUIPMENT

All manner of gadgetry and kitchen equipment was designed to help the housewife in her new kitchen role. Basic household chores, however, did not really change to any great extent and so little was produced to make the work load any lighter.

A batter mixing bowl and an inexpensive brown teapot.

An assortment of flat irons that had to be heated on the kitchen range.

Copper pans with brass handles.

Ceramic bread storage bread crock emblazoned with the miniature maker's name.

Wooden knife cleaner on robust cast-iron stand.

This butter churn is of a traditional design.

Stone storage jars that were filled with preserve would have a piece of cloth tied across the opening secured with a length of string.

A range of cast-iron pots together with a kettle.

ABOVE *The very heart of this British kitchen is the double oven range that sits within a surround complete with mantel shelf. This type of range would have been found in kitchens from about 1890 onwards, but in many ways looks more old-fashioned than its American counterparts. Above the stove is a built-in rack for pan storage or keeping plates or pots warm. The table of clean pine would have its surface scrubbed each day, as this was the main food preparation area.*

THE DRESSER

Once established in the kitchen herself, the Victorian housewife was keen to improve the look of her surroundings. One of the means by which she could do this was by having a dresser. Storage dressers, with open or glazed top shelves, provided display space for decorative crockery or items not regularly in use. At the time grocery producers designed appealing packaging for their products with the intention that they would look attractive on such shelves. All of these items would be within easy reach.

Welsh dresser in "Elizabethan" style displaying a set of the popular willow-ware china.

Glazed china closet for use in the kitchen or pantry.

Pine kitchen dresser with cupboards, drawers, and shelves.

"Hoosier" cabinet with display storage, work surface, and flour bins.

THE STOVE AND ICEBOX

Free-standing stoves and iceboxes were the forerunners of those we know today, but for the Victorians these were the latest designs. The late-nineteenth century was a time of enormous technical and industrial development with an ever-growing market for new products.

The original of this miniature ice-cooled refrigerator was made from 1895 until 1925 by the Belding Hall Company of Belding, Michigan, who owned their own sawmills and made kitchen tables as well.

This excellent miniature stove has been made up from a kit.

A small portable English cottage stove with flue, c. 1900.

Cast-iron range with swing bars and faucet taken from an original made by Smith and Welstood in 1880.

Manufactured by the Richardson and Boynton Company, the original "Perfect" wrought iron single oven range sold in 1890 for $70. The additional shelf was $20. This miniature is made by Handcraft Designs.

Early hand pump for drawing water from a well. It might be located either in the scullery or outside by the back door.

THE SERVANT'S
BEDROOM

In a servant's bedroom, in the attic or the basement, close to the kitchen quarters, it would be unusual to find furnishings that were more than basic. Having no extravagant decoration or comfortable furnishings, these rooms were considered strictly functional and therefore required no more than a cast-iron bedstead, a simple wooden chair, and perhaps a small table, chest, armoire, or other items that were no longer fashionable in the main part of the house. A housekeeper or butler might deserve a little more.

Books on housekeeping advised that hip baths, facilities for writing, a flower vase, and perhaps a picture or text of an enlightening nature might make a servant a little more content.

ABOVE *There is little cheer or comfort to be found in this basic attic room allocated to a lowly maid. Beds of this simple iron construction could be purchased as being suitable for such use. Unfussy and of little decorative merit, their metal construction made them hygienic and easy to keep clean. The mattress was probably made of horsehair.*

THE SERVANT'S FURNITURE

The look of a servant's room might have been somewhat eclectic, with furniture rejected from other parts of the house. Nevertheless there were basic requirements; a bed, a chair, a table, a washstand and perhaps the luxury of a small storage cupboard.

Simple pine side table or washstand, being functional and unadorned.

Perhaps of an older design, trunks like this were still very much in use.

Basic pine stool beautifully made in miniature by David Edwards.

Pine lath-backed chair of about 1833.

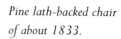

This little pinewood cupboard is strictly utilitarian.

Mass produced in vast quantities, beds of this type became a standard.

A ROOM AT THE TOP

This English attic room is intended for the occupancy of a higher-ranking servant; the personal valet or butler could expect this kind of accommodation as about standard. Furniture is perhaps a little ill-fitting, feasibly rejects from other rooms, but the cast-iron fireplace and enamel-painted bed would have been purposefully chosen for use here.

Nevertheless the room is sparse with little in the way of home comforts. A pitcher and bowl, shaving mirror, travel writing set, hot water bottle, and a few pictures are among the items that are required. The large leather trunk would have contained the occupant's worldly goods or "things," remaining permanently on hand should it be necessary to move on to another post.

Made in the roof space of an actual dollhouse, the character of the room was already determined. A false chimney breast was added to accommodate a fireplace and the wall behind the bed brought forward for extra character. Papering was not quite as easy as before because of the sloping ceiling, but with careful measuring and adjustment it can be done! Flooring is more sheeting, and baseboard was fixed as explained before.

ABOVE *A trunk might be kept at hand in case the servant was asked to move on.*

1 *Armoires very often opened with a single central door.*

2 *This side cupboard probably contained a chamber pot in the compartment below.*

A traveling writing case kept paper and pens in order.

1 *A curved front and solid round wooden knobs were a design feature that was repeated many times on chests of drawers.*

2 *Turned legs and ornamented backs were typical features of a Victorian chair.*

3 *Beds of a simple brass or iron design were mass produced and ideal for less important rooms.*

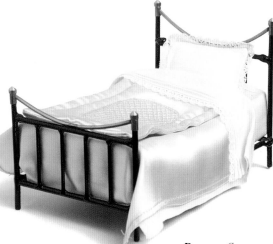

RIGHT *Comparatively comfortable, this bedroom might belong to a higher ranking servant.*

3

HOUSEHOLD CLEANING

Within the field of cleaning, manufacturers came up with numerous inventions intended to make the task easier. Vacuum cleaners, carpet sweepers and all manner of cleaning compounds were available but basic housemaids' boxes, carpet beaters, slop pails and the like were still very much in use.

Two housemaids' boxes with brushes; one made of wood, the other of resin.

Housemaid's cleaning box. The top section lifts out to reveal space for cleaning materials below.

Pail and slop bucket of enameled metal, designed solely for their function.

Early carpet sweeper with handle made of wood.

Early pump action vacuum cleaner which was operated by hand, together with two long-handled shoehorns.

Lovely miniature carpet sweeper finished in wood and brass.

These two miniature carpet beaters have been made using the same technique as real ones.

FIREPLACES

Elaborate fireplaces were important features of a room, frequently demanding attention as the focal point. Before central heating or enclosed stoves, open fires were the only way of heating a room. Every room in the house required one of some sort and in keeping with the time, fire surrounds were available in numerous variations of the latest styles.

Fireplace in Gothic revival style.

Fire surround of an Eastlake influence.

Smaller fireplaces were produced for use in bedrooms.

Marble fireplace surrounds were considered the most impressive.

Elaborate fireplaces were often built into wood-paneled rooms.

Smaller fireplaces than for the rooms downstairs were used for bedrooms, nurseries, and dressing rooms.

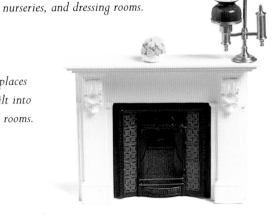

FIREPLACE EQUIPMENT

Being the main necessity in a room, the fireplace demanded much supporting paraphernalia; fire fenders and screens, coal buckets and shovels, brushes to keep the hearth clean and bellows to encourage flames. Sometimes grouped together, fire irons became known as companion sets.

Grates with arched tops became extremely popular.

This companion set might be placed beside the fire ready for use.

Small grates such as this were suitable for bedrooms.

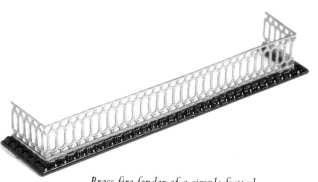

Brass fire fender of a simple fretted design.

Brass fender with leather upholstered "seat."

Parlor stove standing on its stone board. Such a stove would also be used in a family kitchen.

A coal bucket and coal hod for use in the kitchen or just by servants, and a brass coal bucket that could stand in the parlor, dining room, or study.

A coal hod and bucket of polished steel.

ACQUISTO SILVER CO.
8901 Osuna Road, NE
Alburquerque
NM 8711
U.S.A.

SUE AUSTEN
Folley End Farm
Ashton, Bishops Waltham
Hants SO3 1PQ

REUBEN BARROWS
30 Wolsey Gardens
Hainalt
Ilford
Essex IG6 2SN

TOM BATT
Kenton
Beacon Road
Ditchling
East Sussex BN6 8XB

BLACKWELL'S OF HAWKWELL
733–735 London Road
Westcliff-on-Sea
Essex SS0 9ST

DAVID BOOTH
16 Narrabeen Road
Cheriton
Folkestone
Kent CT19 4DD

BRYNTOR
60 Shirburn Road
Torquay
Devon TQ1 4HR

NEIL CARTER
55 Knox Road
Wellingborough
Northants NN8 1JA

TREVOR & SUE COOK
252 Eastern Road
Brighton
East Sussex BN2 5TA

NELL CORKIN
7 Madison Street
Port Washington
NY 11050-3207
U.S.A.

TERRY CURRAN
27 Chapel Street
Mosborough
Sheffield
S. Yorks S19 5BT

ESCUTCHEON
28 Queslett Road East
Streetly, Sutton Coldfield
W. Midlands B74 2EX

FELTON MINIATURES
Field Cottage
Elsthorpe Road
Stainfield
nr Bourne, Lincs PE10 0RS

FLOWERS 'N' THINGS
24 Goldsborough Close
East Leaze, Swindon
Wilts. SN5 7EP

GILLIE'S HANDCRAFTED MINIATURES
37 The Furrows
Walton on Thames
Surrey KT12 3JG

JOHN J. HODGSON
25 Sands Lane
Bridlington
E. Yorkshire YO15 2JG

C.A. & B.A. HOOPER
3 Bunting Close
Ogwell, Newton Abbot
Devon TQ12 6BU

MURIEL HOPWOOD
41 Eastbourne Avenue
Hodge Hill
Birmingham B34 6AR

INTERNATIONAL DOLLS' HOUSE NEWS
Nexus Special Interests Ltd
Nexus House
Boundary Way
Hemel Hempstead
Herts HP2 7ST

TONY KNOTT
Chapel House
Chipping Norton
Oxfordshire OX7 5SZ

KUMMEROWS
P O Box 193
Atascadero
CA 93 423
U.S.A.

CAROL LODDER
Brooks Cottage
Belchalwell
Blandford Forum
Dorset DT11 0EG

MAC DOC DESIGNS
405 Tarrytown Road
No 130
White Plains
New York 10607
U.S.A.

MINIATURE DREAMS
Millbrook Cottage
Carr Moss Lane
Ormskirk
Lancs L39 8SA
U.S.A.

JANE NEWMAN MINIATURES
Linco Cottage
Horningsea
Cambridge CB5 9JG

PHOENIX MODEL DEVELOPMENTS LTD
The Square
Earls Barton
Northampton NN6 0NA

C. & Y. ROBERSON
90 Monmouth Road
Dorchester
Dorset DT1 2DQ

ANNE RUFF
1100 Vagabond Lane
Plymouth
MN 55447
U.S.A.

SUSSEX CRAFTS
Hassocks House
Comptons Brow Lane
Horsham
West Sussex RH13 6BX

THE SINGING TREE
69 New King's Road
London SW6 4SQ

STOKESAY WARE
37 Sandbrook Road
Stoke Newington
London N16 0SH

RAYMOND STOREY
59 Park Crescent
Park Estate
Shiremoor
Newcastle upon Tyne NE27 0LJ

TERENCE & HEATHER STRINGER
Spindles
Lexham Road
Litcham
Norfolk PE32 2QQ

JOE TURNER
13015 N. 49th Place
Scottsdale
AZ 85254
U.S.A.

JIM WATT
Allendale
2 Church Road
Aylmerton
Norfolk NR11 8PS

FRANCIS WHITTMORE
480 Wade Avenue
Lansdale
PA 19446
U.S.A.

WOOD 'N' WOOL
Yew Tree House
3 Stankelt Road
Silverdale
Carnforth
Lancs LA5 0RB

KINDNESS AND COOPERATION FROM:

THE DOLL HOUSE MUSEUM
Station Road
Petworth
West Sussex GU28 0BF

GEFFRYE MUSEUM
Kingsland Road
London E2 8EA

THE GUTHRIE COLLECTION
Hever Castle
nr Edenbridge
Kent TN8 7NG

TOY AND MINIATURE MUSEUM OF KANSAS CITY
5235 Oak Street
Kansas City
MO 64112
U.S.A.

Carole and Barry Kaye
MUSEUM OF MINIATURES
5900 Wilshire Boulevard
Los Angeles
CA 90036
U.S.A.

The Singing Tree
Handcraft Designs
Pamela Cornish

MAKERS OF MINIATURES WHOSE PRODUCTS ARE AVAILABLE THROUGH SPECIALIST SHOPS

Furniture – Bespaq Corporation
Furniture – Handcraft Designs
Furniture Kits – B.H. Miniatures
Furniture Kits – Realife Kits
Handcrafted small items – David Edwards
Lighting – Small Time Operators
Moldings – Northeastern
Wallpaper – Minigraphics